T0339922

HR Due Diligence

CHANDOS
ASIAN STUDIES SERIES:
CONTEMPORARY ISSUES AND TRENDS

Series Editor: Professor Chris Rowley,
Centre for Research on Asian Management, Cass Business School,
City University, UK; HEAD Foundation, Singapore
(e-mail: c.rowley@city.ac.uk)

Chandos Publishing is pleased to publish this major Series of books entitled *Asian Studies: Contemporary Issues and Trends*. The Series Editor is Professor Chris Rowley, Director, Centre for Research on Asian Management, City University, UK and Director, Research and Publications, HEAD Foundation, Singapore.

Asia has clearly undergone some major transformations in recent years and books in the Series examine this transformation from a number of perspectives: economic, management, social, political and cultural. We seek authors from a broad range of areas and disciplinary interests: covering, for example, business/management, political science, social science, history, sociology, gender studies, ethnography, economics and international relations, etc.

Importantly, the Series examines both current developments and possible future trends. The Series is aimed at an international market of academics and professionals working in the area. The books have been especially commissioned from leading authors. The objective is to provide the reader with an authoritative view of current thinking.

New authors: we would be delighted to hear from you if you have an idea for a book. We are interested in both shorter, practically orientated publications (45,000+ words) and longer, theoretical monographs (75,000–100,000 words). Our books can be single, joint or multi-author volumes. If you have an idea for a book, please contact the publishers or Professor Chris Rowley, the Series Editor.

Dr Glyn Jones
Chandos Publishing
E-mail: gjones@chandospublishing.com
www.chandospublishing.com

Professor Chris Rowley
Cass Business School, City University
E-mail: c.rowley@city.ac.uk
www.cass.city.ac.uk/faculty/c.rowley

Chandos Publishing: Chandos Publishing is an imprint of Woodhead Publishing Limited. The aim of Chandos Publishing is to publish books of the highest possible standard: books that are both intellectually stimulating and innovative.

We are delighted and proud to count our authors from such well known international organisations as the Asian Institute of Technology, Tsinghua University, Kookmin University, Kobe University, Kyoto Sangyo University, London School of Economics, University of Oxford, Michigan State University, Getty Research Library, University of Texas at Austin, University of South Australia, University of Newcastle, Australia, University of Melbourne, ILO, Max-Planck Institute, Duke University and the leading law firm Clifford Chance.

A key feature of Chandos Publishing's activities is the service it offers its authors and customers. Chandos Publishing recognises that its authors are at the core of its publishing ethos, and authors are treated in a friendly, efficient and timely manner. Chandos Publishing's books are marketed on an international basis, via its range of overseas agents and representatives.

Professor Chris Rowley: Dr Rowley, BA, MA (Warwick), DPhil (Nuffield College, Oxford) is Subject Group leader and the inaugural Professor of Human Resource Management at Cass Business School, City University, London, UK, and Director of Research and Publications for the HEAD Foundation, Singapore. He is the founding Director of the multi-disciplinary and internationally networked Centre for Research on Asian Management (http://www.cass.city.ac.uk/cram/index.html) and Editor of the leading journal *Asia Pacific Business Review* (http://www.tandf.co.uk/journals/titles/13602381.asp). He is well known and highly regarded in the area, with visiting appointments at leading Asian universities and top journal Editorial Boards in the UK, Asia and the US. He has given a range of talks and lectures to universities, companies and organisations internationally with research and consultancy experience with unions, business and government, and his previous employment includes varied work in both the public and private sectors. Professor Rowley researches in a range of areas, including international and comparative human resource management and Asia Pacific management and business. He has been awarded grants from the British Academy, an ESRC AIM International Study Fellowship and gained a 5-year RCUK Fellowship in Asian Business and Management. He acts as a reviewer for many funding bodies, as well as for numerous journals and publishers. Professor Rowley publishes extensively, including in leading US and UK journals, with over 370 articles, books, chapters and other contributions.

Bulk orders: some organisations buy a number of copies of our books. If you are interested in doing this, we would be pleased to discuss a discount. Please e-mail wp@woodheadpublishing.com or telephone +44 (0) 1993 499140.

HR Due Diligence

Mergers and acquisitions
in China

CHYEKOK HO AND CHINSENG KOH

CP

CHANDOS
PUBLISHING

Oxford Cambridge Philadelphia New Delhi

Chandos Publishing
Hexagon House
Avenue 4
Station Lane
Witney
Oxford OX28 4BN
UK
Tel: +44 (0) 1993 848726
E-mail: info@chandospublishing.com
www.chandospublishing.com

Chandos Publishing is an imprint of Woodhead Publishing Limited

Woodhead Publishing Limited
80 High Street
Sawston
Cambridge CB22 3HJ
UK
Tel: +44 (0) 1223 499140
Fax: +44 (0) 1223 832819
www.woodheadpublishing.com

First published in 2012

ISBN: 978-0-08-101709-8 (print) (Chandos Publishing)
ISBN: 978-0-85709-153-6 (print) (Woodhead Publishing)

ISBN: 978-1-78063-328-2 (online)

British Library Cataloguing-in-Publication Data.
A catalogue record for this book is available from the British Library.

Typeset by RefineCatch Limited, Bungay, Suffolk
Printed in the UK and USA.

For our families:

Lay Beng, William and Wilfred Ho
Whei Kiang, Lynn and Wayne Koh

Contents

List of figures and table

Figures

Table

About the authors

Koh ChinSeng is an experienced senior HR professional with over 30 years of extensive human resource management in several large multinational companies of diverse industries. Organisations that he has worked with include Philips, Thomson multimedia, BOC Gases and Singapore Technologies Aerospace.

His scope of responsibilities spans across South-east Asia to China where he was based in Shanghai and Beijing for the past ten years. Besides the traditional areas of HR portfolio such as Resourcing, Compensation & Benefits Management, Performance Management, Training & Development, Career/Succession Planning and Employee/Industrial Relations, he has built up a reservoir of expertise in the non-traditional segments of HR management to support business growth and sustainability. These areas include conducting HR Due Diligence for M&A activities and HR Risks Assessment, with particular focus on China.

He has jointly delivered a refereed paper on HR Due Diligence to an inaugural business conference to an international audience organized by Australia's Monash University and Beijing's University of International Business and Economics. Moreover, he has also contributed papers relating to the application of change management in China as part of a book edited by Prof Ruth Alas, Estonian Business School, published in 2009.

ChinSeng holds a Bachelor of Arts from the University of Singapore and speaks both English and Chinese fluently.

Dr ChyeKok Ho teaches International Human Resource Management and Management Information Systems at the School of Business, Monash University Sunway Campus in Malaysia. Prior to pursuing a career in academia, he was practice leader and founder of The Knowledge Practice, an organisational research and education advisory business located in Melbourne, Australia.

Dr Ho coached organisational practitioners and business managers on employment processes, professional development interventions, team performance and peer reviews, overseas assignment and reward management and human resource management technologies drawn from multinational corporations, employers federations and labour organisations located in Beijing, Ulaanbaatar, Hanoi, Danang, Ho Chi Minh City, Kuala Lumpur and Singapore.

He has held leadership positions in compensation and benefits management, and was head of human resource for global corporations including investment bank JP Morgan, government-linked conglomerate Singapore Technologies Industrial, and information storage media manufacturer Seagate Technology International.

A researcher in organisation functioning, Dr Ho presented his findings in the areas of human resource due diligence, organiSational learning and knowledge sharing, education pedagogy and technology at peer-reviewed International Business, Knowledge Management, Learning Theories, and Small and Medium Enterprises academic conferences held in Beijing, Hangzhou, Hong Kong, Penang and Singapore.

Dr Ho has degrees from University of Melbourne, Australia, and Cambridge University, United Kingdom. He is an elected Fellow of the Cambridge Commonwealth Society, United Kingdom. His research interests are in the areas of organisational learning and knowledge, knowledge sharing in Chinese communities, and international Human Resource Management.

Preface

We write to share our experience in conducting human resource (HR) due diligence for mergers and acquisitions (M&A) activities in China. Our experiences are gleaned from years of exposure to and personal encounters in conducting HR due diligence in China. As overseas Chinese, we have done plenty, seen a great deal, and have learned not to be presumptuous working with the Chinese and in China.

In a highly complex, and complicated, business environment where intense M&A discussions and effective negotiations take place across different time zones and cultures, intentions are often unseen, left unspoken or tacitly misunderstood. M&A and human resource management practitioners, management consultants, embarking and/or working on M&A related projects as well as graduate scholars of international business, international management, and international human resource management may find our intentions, our exposure to and experience in HR due diligence meaningful and useful. Although our work on HR due diligence may not be intensively grounded on theoretical research methods, with hypotheses rigorously tested, supported, and reliably validated with empirical evidence gathered ethnographically or phenomenologically, we are assured that scholars and academic researchers may nonetheless be keen to learn about our life in the swamp.

Through experiences obtained in diverse industries dispersed across Chinese provinces, we have had our mixed share of joy and pain; successes and setbacks; satisfaction and disappointment. Through the arduous journey of learning and knowing HR due diligence, we have been blind-sighted on many occasions. These oversights provide us with valuable lessons that shape our thinking, and have contributed much to the development of the HR due diligence framework and process. From a China perspective, the purpose is to share our experience in working with the Chinese. The laws or regulations of another, or third, country are not taken into consideration in our writings, especially if these regulations impinge on the conduct of M&A activities in China.

As we learn from our experience in working with the Chinese, we offer several ideas on HR due diligence matters that may appear prescriptive in nature. Our ideas should not be taken as prescriptions for navigating the Chinese M&A landscape, but rather as experience-sharing endeavours situated in context. Prescriptions invariably have their fair share of unseen side-effects as the dosage is never administered properly.

We tell our stories from real-life encounters to illustrate relevant points in the due diligence process. Collectively, we pool diverse experience in the trenches and exposure over years of undertaking M&A in China through the lens of international HR management to make sense of practice. In the chapters that follow, we describe the basic building blocks that are assembled methodically, so that HR due diligence can be conducted systematically and comprehensively.

To do that, we organise the M&A process into three distinct phases, with activities characteristically grouped into upstream, midstream and downstream. All preparatory work, including the formulation of HR strategies, takes place in the upstream phase, signifying the commencement of activities that mark HR support work in the advent of an M&A. Once the preparatory work is complete, the focus shifts towards substantive due diligence work. This is the point where HR due diligence activities reach midstream. Metaphorically, navigating the raging waters of a fast-flowing river requires the expertise of a due diligence team to tame the rapids and torrents zigzagging across the river, and at times against its natural flow and directions. These rapids and torrents represent the risks and frequently unseen costs that are plentiful in an M&A landscape. An inexperienced HR due diligence practitioner may not know the paths that are beset with strong currents. Whether we end up navigating through calm or choppy waters is not the point of contention. Treading the midstream, we encounter the daunting task of uncovering HR-related costs. As we emerge from the rough waters of the midstream, the river will accumulate silt and slows its flow, just as time will heal disagreements and disputes among HR due diligence team members so as to bring warmth and affection to the negotiating parties. This phase marks an entry into downstream. The handing over of the management of the business unit resembles the point where the waters gush into the river mouth and pour into the vastness of an uncharted sea. The vastness of the sea is portrayed by the management integration process.

A major portion of the book has been devoted to guide readers on the areas to search for and/or to scrutinise the underlying segments which are fraught with significant costs implications, if left unseen. HR matters left unseen will not be presented and negotiated as part of M&A transactions. Cost items, if undiscovered, will adversely impact the financial bottom line. The unseen cost items are virtually latent, awaiting an explosive transformation. If the cost items explode after the M&A deal is sealed, the impact on the financial bottom line can be bottomless. This is one area where oversight or negligence can turn out to be a financial nightmare. It may sound paradoxical but if we are compelled to describe the most significant task in conducting HR Due Diligence in China in a single phrase, it is *to see what is unseen.*

The book is also written with the Chinese reader in mind. Translating the script into the Hanyu language may be awkward as organisational sensemaking and the cultural nuances of working with the Chinese and in China may be lost in translation.

This writing would have been impossible if not for the mutually generative discussion we had with academic scholars, colleagues, international business consultants, human resource management practitioners and friends, whose insights and experience on living life in the swamp are documented. We acknowledge, in particular, Mr Steven Fang of The Linde Group, Greater China for granting us access to their archival records on joint venture preparation and negotiations in China. In addition, ChyeKok Ho would like to thank his mum Madam Lim Lee Lee for her unconditional love and support in pursuing his passion for learning-by-doing and knowing-in-practice.

An overview

Abstract: The accession of China into the World Trade Organization (WTO) has paved the way for a phenomenal increase in foreign investments into China. As China opens previously closed industrial and service sectors to foreign direct investments by eliminating operating restrictions imposed on foreign invested enterprises (FIEs), the climate for Mergers and Acquisitions (M&A) as a strategic investment vehicle into China is intensely vibrant, and the marketplace increasingly competitive.

Key words: economic reform, harmonious society, Engel coefficient, direct investment, mergers and acquisitions

China and the Chinese

The People's Republic of China was founded on 1 October 1949 when the Communist Party leader Chairman Mao Zedong proclaimed its conception from the Gate of Heavenly Peace that fronts Tiananmen Square, marking the victory of the Communists over the Kuomintang in the Chinese Civil War. Since then, several significant events have taken place. The years 1956 to 1961 saw the Great Leap Forward Movement, an economic and social campaign of the Chinese Communist Party (CCP) aimed at exploiting its vast population to rapidly transform the country from an agrarian economy into a modern communist society. The movement prohibited private farming and those engaged in it were labelled as counter-revolutionaries and persecuted. As the liberal middle class infiltrated the communist party and society at large to restore capitalism, Mao Zedong launched the Great Proletarian Cultural Revolution to remove the middle class through revolutionary violent class struggle. For ten years from 1966 to 1976, the Chinese people experienced the Cultural Revolution that officially ended with the demise of Mao Zedong. After Mao's death in 1976, Deng Xiaoping, who opposed the Cultural Revolution, gained prominence, became the leader, and abandoned most of the political, economic, and educational reforms of Mao's revolution.

In 1978, Deng Xiaoping launched China's socialist economic reform. Several years later, in 1992, he went on an inspection tour of southern China to revive the economic reform to transform China into a socialist market economy. One of the key statements of Deng Xiaoping's economic reform is that it does not matter what the colour of the cat is, as long as it is able to catch mice.

Against the fast-growing private sector in the 1990s, large-scale state-owned enterprises (SOEs) were failing. Reforming SOEs was a national agenda. According to Tong (2007), the first phase of the reform was to establish and strengthen profitability-related incentives for the managers, and the second phase was to nurture the big SOEs while letting go of the smaller SOEs. The second wave of SOE reforms resulted in the mass laying off of workers in the urban areas, and the slow and consistent shrinking of the SOEs' share in China's industrial sector. Reforming SOEs created social discontent and disharmony among the Chinese people. Many workers took to the streets to demonstrate against the government.

In 1997, China entered a period of administration by Jiang Zemin and Premier Zhu Rongji. Jiang and Zhu oversaw

China's accession to the World Trade Organization (WTO) in 2001. Then, there were fears among some of China's economic sectors as China opened its domestic markets to the world. Such fears were judged unfounded as the Chinese leadership successfully integrated China into the world economy. Hu Jintao assumed the party leadership in 2002. In addressing income disparity, gaps between urban and rural development, occupational health and safety in SOEs, state corruption and environmental protection, Hu adopted a humane style of leadership and, at the same time, enhanced state authority and control. His balanced approach, Wang and Lye (2007) argue, is embodied in the 'Three people's principles': power to be used by the people; concern to be showered on the people; and benefits to be enjoyed by the people. The 'three people's principles' have eventually been manifested in the concept of an 'harmonious society'. An 'harmonious society', according to Hu Jintao, would contain elements of fairness and uprightness, rule of law, order, democracy and balance between the needs of man and nature. In 2008, seven years after China's accession to the WTO, Chinese foreign exchange reserves exceeded US$1.9 trillion, boosting China's confidence in leading its economy in a globalised world. As of 2009, Chinese gross domestic product (GDP) ranked third globally and China overtook Germany to become the world's biggest exporter.

Geographically, China is the third largest country in the world, after Canada and Russia, with a land area of approximately 9.6 million square kilometres, covering 6.7 per cent of the world's surface area. As of 2008, its population is 1.328 billion, with more than 90 million Chinese living in the Henan (94.29 million), Shangdong (94.17 million), and Guangdong (95.44 million) regions. In its major cities, there are approximately 17 million people living in Beijing, 19 million in Shanghai, 10 million in

Guangzhou, and about 9 million in Shenzhen. The largest municipality/city is Chongqing with a population of 28.39 million. The eastern part of China is more densely populated than the western part. The average household size in 2008 is 3.16 people. The population growth on a year-on-year basis has reduced from 12 per cent in 1978 to 5.08 per cent in 2008. According to Reuters (2008), the Chinese population is expected to grow to 1.5 billion by 2033.

As of 2008, the median age of the Chinese is 34.1 years. There are about 105 males to 100 females. China has about 150 million people aged 60 or above, comprising 11.6 per cent of its population; the old age dependency stands at 10 per cent. According to the United Nations Procurement Division, this figure is projected to increase to 39 per cent by 2050.

The Han ethnicity makes up the majority 92 per cent of the population, with 55 ethnic minorities accounting for the remaining 8 per cent. The major dialects are Beiyu, Minyu, Xiangyu, Yueyu, Keyu and Ganyu. Its diverse population are spread across five autonomous regions (Guangxi, Xinjiang, Tibet, Inner Mongolia and Ningxia); 22 provinces (Hebei, Shanxi, Liaoning, Jilin, Heilongjiang, Jiangsu, Zhejiang, Anhui, Fujian, Jiangxi, Shandong, Henan, Hubei, Hunan, Guangdong, Hainan, Sichuan, Guizhou, Yunnan, Shaanxi, Gansu and Qinghai); and four municipalities (Beijing, Shanghai, Tianjin and Chongqing). The 31 autonomous regions, provinces and municipalities are under the direct control of the central government.

The urban population, i.e. those living in cities and towns, accounted for approximately 45 per cent, so the rural population is 55 per cent. In 1978, the year the reform policy was promulgated by Deng Xiaoping, the ratio of urban to rural population was 17.9 per cent to 82.1 per cent. This ratio increased to 26.4 per cent and 73.6 per cent respectively in 1990. By 2000, the gap between urban and rural was narrowed to 36.2 per cent and 63.8 per cent. The shift in the urban to rural population may not have any historical significance in terms of its sheer numbers in the labour movement. However, the increase in urban population reflected a higher economic growth rate which was sustained over a period coupled with internal labour movements. It was reported that 130 million migrant workers uprooted themselves from their home towns in the rural provinces to the cities in search of work and better earning opportunities; initially drawn to the first-tier coastal cities and subsequently to the second-tier cities. According to *China Daily* (2009), there are more than 240 million unemployed urban residents in China.

Currently, China has more than 118 megalopolises with a population exceeding 1 million each and 39 super metropolises of more than 2 million residents each. Overall, the standard of living, measured by the Engel coefficient, of the urban and rural population has improved significantly, and the gap between urban and rural Engel coefficient has narrowed over the past 30 years. The Engel coefficient of the urban population in 2008 was 37 per cent, and that of the rural population was 43.7 per cent. In 1978, the Engel coefficient for urban population was 57.5 per cent, and for rural population 67.7 per cent.

According to *China Daily* (2009), China invests 2.8 per cent of its gross domestic product (GDP) in education as compared to the OECD countries' investment of 5 per cent of GDP. The literacy rate in China increased from 84.12 per cent in 1990 to 93.3 per cent in 2008, and 72 per cent of the senior school graduates in 2008 went on to tertiary education. Of postgraduate enrolments, 59,764 are doctoral candidates, and 386,658 are studying for a Master's degree. The disciplines studied by postgraduate candidates are engineering, medicine, management, law and economics. In addition, literature is popular at graduate level. In 2009, there were more than 1.28 million postgraduates and Chinese students studying abroad. Three hundred million Chinese people were reported to be learning English in China and approximately 40 million students were learning Chinese outside of China.

A recent report by IDP Education Australia commented that China is adding 2.5 million domestic tertiary education places annually, representing a 25 per cent compound annual growth rate. However, demand for university places continues to outstrip supply. It is estimated that 350,000 mainland Chinese are studying for degrees in overseas universities and the number is expected to double within the next 20 years. There were an estimated 120,000 Chinese students studying in Australia in 2009 and 23,000 Chinese students were granted British student visas in 2007. Among the international students overseas, Chinese students at overseas universities exceeded all other nationalities. The reason, IDP Education reported, for the large number of Chinese students overseas is the lack of university places in the home country; opportunities for skilled migration; perceptions of improved employment and career prospects for overseas graduates; and the beliefs about better quality education and overseas life experiences.

From the economic data for 2007, the size of China's economy is approximately US$3.26 trillion, which lags a long way behind the GDP of the US at US$13.84 trillion in 2007. China's share of global GDP stands at 7.14 per cent in year 2008, compared to 1.8 per cent at the time of the economic reform policy of Deng Xiaoping in 1978. Since then, more than 200 million of the Chinese people have been lifted out of poverty. Fogel (2010), an economics Nobel laureate, predicted that China's GDP in the year 2040 will increase to US$123 trillion; capturing a 40 per cent share of global GDP, larger than the US share of 14 per cent and the European Union share of 5 per cent.

When Deng Xiaoping took over the leadership from Mao Zedong, China's foreign exchange reserves stood at US$1.6 billion. Ten years later, in 1997, these reserves were US$139.9 billion, lagging behind the Asian economies of Taiwan, Hong Kong and Singapore. By the year 2001, the reserves exceeded US$200 billion. As at the end of February 2010, China's foreign exchange reserves exceeded US$2 trillion. With a GDP that is growing phenomenally, China is becoming the world's largest economy. Huge foreign exchange reserves would have a significant impact on Outflow of Direct Investments (ODI) and/or Foreign Direct Investment (FDI) and Merger and Acquisition (M&A) transactions. Perhaps there will be an increase in cross-border M&A transactions, both from inbound and outbound direct investments of the Chinese and China.

An AT Kearney report on 'The Rise of Emerging Markets in Mergers & Acquisitions' concluded that 'a paradigm shift is occurring [in that] beginning in 2002, deals between developing and developed countries grew at an annual rate of 19 per cent'. In another study on 'Mergers & Acquisitions: impacts of WTO Accession', Chen and Shi (2008) observe that 'among M&A markets worldwide, the Asia Pacific region has normally accounted for only 15 per cent of all M&A transactions worldwide. But in 1H05 [first half of 2005], this figure reached 18 per cent'. AT Kearney reported that of the 2,168 major acquisitions in 2007 between developed and developing countries, almost 20 per cent were driven by companies from developing countries; this trend is growing at an annual rate of 26 per cent. Their study concluded that companies from India, Malaysia and China are at the forefront of M&A activities, accounting for 56 per cent of the deals which took place between 2002 and

2007. Moving away from the region and focusing on China specifically, there were 63 cross-border M&A transactions in 2007 with a value of US$18.67 billion, an increase of 105.4 per cent over the previous year. In 2008, the value of M&A deals increased by 44 per cent, followed by 135 inbound transactions into China totalling US$10.6 billion in 2009. Looking at M&A from a different perspective, the *China Foreign Investment Report* 2006 commented 'Mergers and acquisitions have emerged as a common channel for global investments since the 1990s, accounting for nearly 80 per cent of the total worldwide. But they currently account for less than 10 per cent of total foreign direct investments to China'. It appears there is a large amount of scope for inbound M&A into China in the coming years.

M&A activities in China

As of the mid-1990s, M&A transactions in China were relatively unnoticed. At present, the situation is one where mergers and acquisitions are becoming increasingly common and form an integral part of the economic landscape. Two major factors may be responsible for the surge of M&A activities in China. The first is the economic reforms which were promulgated in 1978 by Deng Xiaoping that led to decades of high economic growth, and the second is China's accession to the WTO in 2001. China's economic reforms and phenomenal economic growth fuelled the rate of M&A activities, and its accession to the WTO opened its hitherto closed door to foreign investments. The economic landscape was quickly transformed from a centrally-planned to a market-driven economy. In the 1980s, investments were mainly restricted to export-oriented joint ventures with Chinese firms. As the country moved into the early

1990s, foreign enterprises were allowed to produce goods for sale in the domestic Chinese market. By the mid-1990s, the rules and regulations on foreign investments into China were relaxed to permit wholly foreign owned enterprises (WFOEs) to set up their operations locally.

Concurrent with the economic reforms, China also restructured its state-owned assets. In several industrial sectors, the state encouraged its state-owned enterprises (SOEs) to merge into gigantic conglomerates to compete in the global marketplace by exploiting their core business, while in other sectors it sought to reduce its equity holding. As a result, large numbers of SOEs were made available for restructuring and/or partnership with foreign entities. These potential targets therefore represent greater market entry options to foreign investors.

Undoubtedly, China's entry into the WTO is the catalyst that compelled the Chinese government to open the service sector to the world, thereby paving the way for foreign investors to operate in domestic markets. These developments served to open up previously closed industrial and service sectors to foreign investments by eliminating operating restrictions that were previously imposed on foreign invested enterprises. The opening up of the domestic sectors attracted inflows of FDI exploiting M&A as a strategic vehicle for foreign investors. M&A offers foreign investors a convenient and effective platform to gain knowledge and market share as well as to jump-start and accelerate expansion of their business. An analysis frequently touted is that foreign acquisition of or participation in listed or non-listed enterprises or SOEs, especially in sectors which were previously out-of-bounds to foreign investments, would become more frequent, especially in the financial services and telecommunications sectors, resulting in greater consolidation of the industry. Research on legal and financial services set-ups in China confirms that M&A as a trend will continue in the coming years. Such is the optimistic mood that is widely prevalent among M&A commentators in their respective fields: legal counsel, financial experts, management integration consultants and/or scholars.

With increasing open-handed investment opportunities and a pervasive sense of optimism, it may be possible and perhaps feasible to translate significant FDIs into M&A activities. Notwithstanding the more optimistic outlook among the specialist community at large and China's determination to relentlessly pursue a market driven economy and its willingness to comply with international standards and practices, China remains steadfastly a socialist state with meticulously planned economic influences. Above all, government policies are inclined towards and favour social stability and control. Transacting in China, Hodgson (2008) cautions, can be a minefield. From this crisp message, one can surmise that Hodgson is implying that the M&A journey in China is full of treacherous potholes, into which an unsuspecting investor can easily fall. Hodgson adds, 'Risks are capable of being identified and mitigated if the right people are charged with the responsibility of undertaking due diligence'. The key to success lies in having or finding the 'right people' with the appropriate competencies to carry out the task of the unknown, unseen and the unconventional. This point will be more closely examined when we move to the chapters on HR risk assessment and managing integration.

2

Cultivating affective relationships

Abstract: Cultivating affective relationship by building guānxi is a pre-requisite in managing the Human Resource Due Diligence process. The notion of guānxi is unpacked into human-heartedness; affection; appointed trust; usefulness of trust; personality; and face in society. The importance of social exchanges of favours; dynamic positioning of social hierarchies; and the intricate balancing of power are emphasised in M&A negotiations. For the Chinese people, the law is not beyond humaneness.

Key words: guānxi, human-heartedness, affection, appointed trust, face, social hierarchies, humaneness

Relations and relationships

In Western economies, business is generally conducted within rules-based systems under laws that are widely known and justly enforced. In contrast, business conducted in China is based on personal contacts and relationships. The Chinese have an aversion to formal, written contracts and prefer to rely on personal relations, and social contacts with those in power to get things done. Chinese businessmen typically start with a bare skeleton of written agreements and rules, leaving the rest to negotiation and oral interpretation as the business relationship evolves. Personal connections and loyalties are often more important than organisational affiliations or legal standards. Business is transacted within a relation-based system, supposedly made on the strength and interpretations of verbal agreements anchored on trust.

In building affective relationships, there are two Chinese concepts which can be used as management precepts. The first one, guānxi, is well known in the Westernised world. The second concept, *He Qíng* (合情), *He Li* (合理), *HeFa* (合法) is less well known, especially among Westerners. *Guānxi* means connection and/or network. *QíngLiFa* (情理法) can be interpreted as 'in conformity with the context of the given situation, in conformity with the principle of reasonableness and in conformity with prevailing laws and regulations'. From an application of the ideas in terms of its use, or usefulness, guānxi can be said to be externally pulled whereas *QíngLiFa* is internally driven. In building relationships or networks which facilitate business processes, the sources of influence are all external, whether they are the regulatory authorities, permit-granting authorities, bureaux, business/project partners, key suppliers, joint venture partners or customers. In managing Chinese employees, *QíngLiFa* can be relied upon as a core management principle as it embodies the traditional values and societal values more than the Chinese as a people have imbibed. If one were to examine the Chinese culture and study the manner in which matters are viewed, one will find that the Chinese are inclined to consider all three factors, qíng, li and fa holistically, and one aspect of an idea is never considered without the others. *Qíng* is considered to be the foundation and *li* is the key to resolving issues. This is the case as qíng and *fa* need *li* to achieve the level of clarity and understanding of any given situation. *Qíng* without *li* is tantamount to being ruled by emotions whereas *fa* without *li* is a case of a bad law being enacted.

Guānxi (关系)

The Chinese word *guānxi* is a combination of guān (关) and xi (系). According to the *Xian Dai Han Yu Ci Dian* (现代汉语词典 or *Modern Chinese Dictionary*), *guān* means 'door' with an extended meaning 'to close up'. *Xi* means 'to connect and enter into relationships' as in kinship. As a metaphor, guānxi suggests, 'you may be one of us if you are inside the door that we have closed; but if you are outside the door, you are not one of us'. It implies 'the old boy network' of public schools in Western societies; the clans and triads in Chinese businesses, or 'the inner circles' of a government's members.

As a concept, *guānxi* refers to the drawing on connections in order to secure favours in personal relations. It is an aspect of the Chinese business practice whereby individuals are able to establish a complex network of assistance. *Guānxi* is an intricate and pervasive relational network that the Chinese cultivate energetically, subtly, and imaginatively (Luo, 1997). Historically, it was Chinese merchants seeking informal mechanisms and 'backdoor' relationships to secure the kind of transactions often protected by law that gave rise to the idea of *guānxi*. *Guānxi* provided a balance to the cumbersome government bureaucracy by allowing people to circumvent rules and regulations through the activation of personal relations. In this respect, guānxi operated with some success in place of the law of the land that was often unclear, biased, unreliable, and in constant flux.

The idea of *guānxi* originates from the early days in China. Living under harsh conditions, Chinese peasants continually experienced famine and starvation. With limited resources, lives were extremely difficult and uncertain. Scarce resources were allocated according to whom you knew. Reliance on one's family resources was not sufficient. It was necessary to extend one's familial form of support through kin and distant relations, membership of a village community, and work groups. The method of extending familial support beyond one's family came to be known as guānxi.

Guānxi are established in places where there are Chinese communities. For example, when the Chinese came to Southeast Asia in search of work, they arrived on their own without their families or kin. Fresh off the boats, the new arrivals turned to people originally from their villages in China for food, lodging, and work. They sought support by 'connecting' to groups that were organised along the lines of their dialects; the villages they originally came from, or ancestry as in having the same family name. If they were not able to locate their groups, they would get in touch with intermediaries to connect them to help groups. Access to help groups was based on the personal recommendations of intermediaries. Referrals were important for 'peripherals to legitimately participate in communities of *guānxi*'. As membership of these communities grew, mutual help groups were institutionalised as clans, and trade associations.

Through social activities, clans and trade associations created opportunities for the migrant Chinese to establish *guānxi* with potential traders and bankers. Chinese migrants found work mostly through the *guānxi* channels. In addition, the Chinese *towkay* (businessmen and employers) strengthened their networks of dependable guānxi by binding capable workers to their businesses through marriages.

Hence, *guānxi* became a web of networks that encompasses a broad range of relationships and kinships. Individuals are encouraged to develop relationships of respect and responsibility. *Guānxi* was modelled on filial piety, relationship between spouses, and traditional family values underpinned by Confucian ideals.

The key themes that are intricately linked to the core concept of *guānxi* are emotion, trust and face. As the Chinese have a tendency to follow their hearts more than their heads, the building of relationships is predominantly an emotive process. Such emotive processes are bounded by two closely-knit ideas: *rénqíng* (human-heartedness – 人情); and *gǎnqíng* (affection – 感情). *Rénqíng* may be defined as felt experience gained through social exchange of favours. It connotes a mental state of indebtedness as a consequence of 'securing a favour from someone' with moral and social obligations of reciprocity. *Gǎnqíng* translated literally means affection. Affection, as defined in *The Shorter Oxford Dictionary*, is 'an emotion, a feeling and a disposition towards something'. From a *guānxi* perspective, *gǎnqíng* connotes goodwill generated through exchanges of favours in social encounters and feelings towards one another cultivated over a period of time.

Trust refers to the 'willingness of a person to accept vulnerability based on positive expectations of another's intentions or behaviours' (Mayer et al., 1995; Rousseau et al., 1998). Tong and Yong (1998) stated that a Chinese business person is more interested in whether a person will deal honestly with him in particular. This willingness is influenced by the pre-existence of *guānxi*. If there is no pre-existing *guānxi*, the reluctance of the business person to undertake risk is higher. The business person could really only build up xìnyong after s/he has first established *guānxi*. For a peripheral participant in a community of *guānxi*, it is more of a presumption of trust, as the person proceeds to establish his *xìnyong* with his actions (Tong and Yong, 1998: 85).

The notion of trust (*xìn* – 信) signifies *xìnrèn* (appointed trust – 信任) and *xìnyong* (use or usefulness of personal trust – 信用). The *Concise Oxford Chinese–English Dictionary* (1999) defines *rèn* (任) as 'to formally appoint, or to assume a position'. In the context of *guānxi*, *xìnrèn* may be interpreted as personal trust sanctioned by the community. *Xìnyong*, which is interpreted as the use or usefulness of *xìnrèn*, is instrumental in securing favours through social exchanges. It symbolises the reputation of a person in relation to its creditability and trustworthiness. In building personal relationships, social exchanges of favours will strengthen rénqíng and enhance *xìnyong*.

Although *xìnyong* is personal trust, it is also a social practice. Trust is an essential part of a dynamic relationship, and an aspect of culture that requires cultivation (Solomon and Flores, 2001; Abrams et al., 2003). *Xìnyong* dictates that if a person violates the personal trust that he has established, this person may be ostracised. Members from the *guānxi* network would spread the word that that person has failed to keep his word. His *guānxi* 'door' may be closed to him and he may no longer be 'one of us'. However, the principle of *guānxi* also demands that one should be understanding, flexible, and that compromises can and should be made. Hence, the stronger the *guānxi*, the greater the chances of a violation being forgiven or dismissed as an error of judgement.

Xìnyong can be foolish, naïve, gullible, blind, and may be taken for granted. In a *guānxi* network where there is inequality of status, there may be a tendency for people, because of respect for authority, obedience, loyalty, fear, to be polite and to pretend that there is *xìnyong* even when there is none. Without *xìnyong*, people will continue with their work, they will not offer their ideas, will refrain from criticising what they perceive as bad ideas or their bosses, and courteously agree with things they know cannot possibly work.

In her research on the Chinese concept of face in social settings, Hu (1944) postulates a pair of ideas: *liǎn* (personality – 脸) and *miànzi* (face in society – 面子). Liǎn represents personal qualities rooted in ethics and integrity. It characterises the moral status of a person that may be lost through unacceptable conduct. The person with *liǎn* fulfils unpaid obligations with decency, regardless of hardships and difficulties. A person that *diūliǎn* (to lose face) has not conducted him/herself in accordance with the precepts of the Chinese culture, thereby creating mistrust and strains in *guānxi*. *Miànzi* symbolises prestige; a reputation that is achieved 'getting through in life, through success or ostentation, and accumulated by means of personal effort or clever manoeuvring' (Hu, 1944). Prestige varies according to the community a person interacts with and is dependent at all times on the external environment. In this context, miànzi symbolises the social face and currency of a person in society.

The dynamics of *guānxi* necessitates an intricate balance between not losing one's own face and at the same time saving the face of others. The notions of 'to lose face' and 'to save face' are separate social processes resulting in different outcomes in a social encounter (Ho, 1976). *Diūliǎn* implies the degradation in moral standards of a person as a result of the person conducting him/herself in a socially disagreeable manner.

Culturally, there is no exact translation of the phrase 'to save face' into Hanyu. An understanding of the interrelated concepts of face, which are *yàomiànzi* (to want face), *gùmiànzi* (to consider face), *gěimiànzi* (to give face), and *liúmiànzi* (to leave face) may provide a semantic interpretation of face and face work. Hu (1944) suggests that *yàomiànzi* is the closest approximation of 'to save face'. A person who wants face for oneself strives to 'show that s/he is better situated, more capable, possesses better social connections or a better character than actually is the case' (Hu, 1944). Similarly, a person who *gùmiànzi* for oneself does so to advance his/her own prestige. For *guānxi* to strengthen, saving the face of others is important. As such, *gùmiànzi* takes on a specific meaning, which is to consider the feelings of others by not divulging their vulnerability. In order to *gùmiànzi* to someone, the person may *gěimiànzi* to prevent erosion in prestige and reputation of that person. It is regarded as essential 'not to touch the prestige of a person, not to ruin his reputation, for though the punishment be justified, the sudden loss of prestige built up through years of effort might be too much of a shock for the personality' (Hu, 1944). For a person to *gěimiànzi* (give face) to someone, s/he will have to *liúmiànzi* (to leave face) for that someone. A person may *liúmiànzi* for someone by not commenting openly and/or exposing mistakes made by that person, thus allowing him/her the opportunity to 'save face'.

Guānxi supports the concepts of *gěimiànzi* and *liúmiànzi* in that people should be flexible, understanding, and that compromises can and should be made; the stronger the *guānxi*, the higher the chances of a future violation being forgiven or dismissed as an error of judgement. The act of not losing one's face (*diūliǎn*) and at the same time saving someone's face (*gùmiànzi*) by giving face (*gěimiànzi*) and leaving face (*liúmiànzi*) to that individual add to cultivating guānxi.

Reciprocity is a necessary and sufficient condition for establishing and cultivating *guānxi*. Building a relationship through *guānxi* requires the reciprocation of emotion (*rénqíng* and *gǎnqíng*); development of mutual trust (*xìnrèn* and *xìnyong*); and the saving of face (*liǎn* and *miànzi*) in society. Chinese businessmen, Luo (1997) argues, 'build the relationship first and, if successful, business transactions will follow, whereas Western businesses focus on the commercial aspects of transactions and if they are successful, a relationship may develop'. *Guānxi* must be managed with care or it can become a liability. Warren et al. (2004) added that 'in theory, relationships can both benefit and harm the society, but in practice when a kind of relationship network is established, it will guarantee the privileges of certain groups of people and therefore damage the social justice'. Being attentive to the negative effects of *guānxi*, Vanhonacker (2004) advised 'you can head off relationships that could work against you'.

Building a relationship by building *guānxi* is the first step in managing the Human Resource Due Diligence process. Initial contacts with the Chinese are essential for building rapport and establishing mutual trust and respect. Building *guānxi* requires the social exchange of favours, dynamic positioning of social hierarchies continually, and the intricate balancing of power. Participation in the community of *guānxi* through practice enables the due diligence resource members to gain a fuller understanding of the costs of conducting business, the effectiveness and efficiency of Chinese management systems, and its social and work habits. Shared meanings among members will strengthen *guānxi* and are beneficial in uncovering unseen business costs, facilitate affective negotiations, and manage merger integration.

Using the concept of sets and set theory, the core concept of *guānxi* is symbolically represented in Figure 2.1 as Venn diagrams. As a set, *guānxi* is list-defined as emotion, trust and face. The members or the sub-sets of emotion

Figure 2.1   Core concepts of guānxi

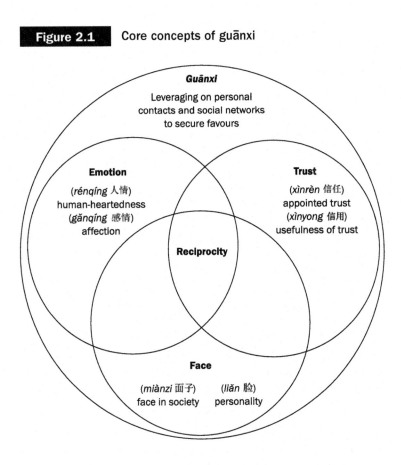

are *rénqíng* and *gǎnqíng*; sub-sets of trust are *xìnrèn* and *xìnyong*; and of face are *liǎn* and *miànzi*. Reciprocity is rule-defined by the intersection of a collection of ideas encapsulating emotion, trust and face. The area of intersection is the element in common that overlaps the notion of reciprocation of emotion, trust and face. In this respect, the unpaid obligations in social exchange of favours, developing mutual trust, and 'to save and/or to lose' face are important elements for cultivating *guānxi*. In addition, set theory defines the relationship linking the elements of the sub-sets to a set. For example, gănqíng may be positively correlated to *xìnyong*; the stronger the emotion, the higher the level of trust.

He Qíng (合情)

Of these three terms, '*qíng, li, fa*', qíng is the most difficult to grapple with. Loosely translated, it can be equated with 'a human dimension', which entails two aspects: one that deals with the context of a given situation and the other to do with humaneness in the way in which the given situation is handled or managed. In order to describe the term *qíng* adequately, an effective way is to relate a couple of cases as metaphors.

When Deng Xiaoping outmanoeuvred Hua Guo Feng, Mao's anointed leader, and took over the mantle of China's leadership in 1978, he inherited a country that was filled with institutions that were politically driven and were a hindrance to growth. At that point, China was economically a minion crawling at a virtually standstill pace. As China is a communist society, it was deeply embedded in political ideology, and Deng could not be seen to abandon the credo of socialism in pursuit of growth along a path of capitalism. Communist theory, as pronounced by Marx, is predicated upon viewing history as a series of continuous class struggles. Under capitalism, the class struggle would be between those who own the means of production, that is, the ruling class which is the bourgeoisie, and the working class who strive to make ends meet by earning a wage, that is, the proletariat. The eventual outcome of the class struggle as envisioned by Marx was that the proletarians will emerge to power through class struggle and revolution against the bourgeoisie. The ultimate society will be one which is classless, and communism holds the key to class equality.

How did Deng overcome this bind of class struggle? He played a masterstroke by coining a new concept termed 'socialism with Chinese characteristics'. Deng rationalised that planning and market forces were not the underlying differences between socialism and capitalism. Just as there is planning under capitalism, there is a market economy under socialism. What Deng was doing was to justify to both his political foes and his allies that he remained steadfastly committed to the ideals of socialism whilst relentlessly pursuing his vision of growth. According to Deng, socialism cannot be equated with poverty; on the contrary, socialism is the elimination of poverty. Among his quotable quotes is to 'let some people get rich first'. This inherently promotes inequality within the ranks of society and certainly runs against the ideals of communism, which aim at transformation into a classless society. Furthermore, allowing private ownership of the means of production also runs contrary to the fundamental precept of Marxist theory as private ownership of the means of production is a basis of capitalism. In fact, commentators concluded that the economic theory as pursued in China is not socialism with Chinese characteristics, but the diametric opposite, 'capitalism with Chinese characteristics'. In the midst of all these apparent contradictions, one sees tacit acceptance of Deng's socialism model. It is inconceivable that Deng could have promoted these ideals or socialist principles during the Cultural Revolution and managed to gain acceptance within the governing circles. The Communist Party hardliners were in abundance and the general apprehensiveness against Western-style capitalist practices was still deeply ingrained.

Naisbitt and Naisbitt eloquently explain the turnaround in thinking and acceptance by the Chinese. In their writing, they quote Zhang Wei Wei as 'The Chinese believe in performance legitimacy. If the government governs well, it is perceived as legitimate'. Transposing these comments onto the socialism of Deng, one realises that the Chinese society, both ruling and working class, must have perceived that his ideas on socialism bring great benefits to its people, which equates with performance, to the Chinese society. To this day, the government of the People's Republic of China still maintains that it has not abandoned Marxism, but has simply developed many of the terms and concepts of Marxist theory to accommodate its new economic system. The fact that it was widely accepted and supported shows its success, but the fact that it remains relevant to this day is an attestation to the enduring vision of Deng.

The illustration of Deng's socialism as a case is primarily due to the fact that in the Chinese language, this case centres on the concept of *guoqíng* (国情) which means extraneous circumstances which the state is in, and this is the context from which state matters must be viewed from the perspective of the Chinese central government. This is similar to the essence of *qíng* in *QíngLiFa*.

Just in case any reader should harbour any impression that *he qíng* represents the art of situating an appreciation rather than appreciating the situation, we think it timely here to introduce the notion of PEA, which is an acronym of perception, expectation and acceptance. Before a person gains acceptance from the Chinese, the person needs to take pains to ensure that whatever concept, scheme, change, policy, system, announcement or objective s/he wishes to attain, the first thing is to take care of the potential perception that the plan or action will likely create in the process of implementation. Even assuming that there was no wrongful or negative perception being created, there is the additional angle of expectation to be careful of. Lofty expectations can only result in unfulfilled hopes which will in turn cause discontentment. This translates into non-acceptance.

He Li (合理)

Li, in the Chinese language, means reasonableness. In the Chinese culture, the concept of reasonableness is very central to one's actions or behaviour. If an action or behaviour is seen by the Chinese to be motivated by unreasonable means, they will view it as wrongful and unacceptable. What then defines reasonableness? Are there measurable standards or widely accepted norms that define the boundaries of reasonableness, outside of which matters will be perceived as unreasonable? Whether an action, decision, scheme, instruction, policy, change or whatever the issue at hand, is considered to be reasonable has to depend on the rationale, basis of comparison, standards and factors applied to the process. Whether it is a case of rationalising one's actions, or making comparisons to determine if one has attained the required standards or deciding on the appropriate factors to apply, it hinges on the basis or assumptions that are being adopted at the outset. Whether these are accepted as fair and reasonable will ultimately depend on whether one has taken into account the vested interests of all parties when deliberating on the issues.

He Fa (合法)

Fa, in the Chinese language, means law or regulation. The Chinese understand that a society that is governed by the rule of law will lead to social harmony. But the concept of the rule of law as understood by the Chinese is different from the way a Westernised person understands it. To the Chinese, a society is complex and s/he sees a legal system as having limitations. How does a person perceive it in such a manner? By nature, real-life situations are seen as being multifarious. Besides the need for a legal system to harmonise and stabilise society, one also needs *qíng* and *li* to supplement the application of the legal system to achieve a semblance of fair play. A case that is often quoted is that in the past, schools were encouraged to organise extra-curricular activities after designated school hours. There was an instance in a spring-time school outing when an accident happened. What followed was that the family of the victim sued the school in a court of law for mismanaging the activity and was awarded compensation. As a consequence, all primary, secondary and high schools abandoned all spring outings in order to avoid potential mishaps, unnecessary inconveniences or costs. Today in China, school children may no longer enjoy this privilege of a springtime school outing. From a strict legal standpoint, the Chinese accepted that the school was liable for damages paid to the victim's family. From a real-life standpoint, the pertinent question that the Chinese would ask is how a school goes about managing this responsibility. Surely, it must be obvious that this is an impossible task for any school to control, let alone be held accountable for? All actions inherently carry an element of risk and there is no such thing as absolutely risk-free. Even if a teacher is assigned to look after a child for 24 hours, there is no guarantee that a mishap will not occur. Once a mishap occurs, it will be doubtful what the principal can effectively do.

For the Chinese, the court adjudging liability against the school is in conformity with the law; but it does not satisfy the principles of *qíng* and *li*. At a personal level, the judgment by the court is perceived to bring relief and consolation to the victim's family, but at a macro level, it is seen to be causing harm to teachers and students alike. This ruling was passed more than ten years ago, resulting in hundreds of millions of Chinese school students no longer being able to enjoy any springtime outings. The Chinese debated this issue hypothetically without knowing if the injury suffered by the victim or the collective impact suffered by subsequent generations of students is greater. This case drives home one lesson to the Chinese and that is that the legal aspect is only one angle and may not be the most important. To a Chinese, if one resolves an issue solely from a legal standpoint, this will be perceived as narrow-minded and prejudiced. It is from this perspective that *qíng*, *li* and *fa* are organised in a consecutive order, and qíng takes precedence over fa. Hence, the phrase '*qíng*, *li* and *fa*' must be understood in that order and the items in the three terms must never be swapped or interchanged in position: *qíng* takes first position, followed by *li* and then *fa*.

How did such thinking come about? There is a Chinese saying 法律无外乎人情, which can be translated to mean 'the law is not beyond humaneness'. This implies that humane or people considerations should supersede the law. Such thinking is definitely at odds with the Westernised concept of the rule of law, which dictates that the law is supreme where dispute resolution is subject to governing laws and regulations. It does not imply that Westernised laws do not take humaneness into consideration. In a Western legal environment, there is segregation between the elements of judgment and of sentencing, once a guilty verdict is passed. The humane factor only comes in when a mitigation plea is being entered upon a verdict being passed. In the Chinese context, however, the two elements are considered concurrently. In a Western legal system, judgment is about compliance with the prevailing law and any breach of it will render a person liable to a guilty verdict. Sentencing is about fairness in the sense that the severity of a wrongdoing will result in a heavier sentence being meted out, with mitigating circumstances to lessen the severity. This is probably the one area which can explain the divergence in viewpoints between the way a Chinese and a Western-oriented person would perceive an outcome of a given legal case.

3

Introducing HR due diligence

Abstract: The phases of a Human Resource Due Diligence process in mergers and acquisition (M&A) transactions may be clustered into upstream; midstream; and downstream. Amongst the key factors to consider are the formulation of appropriate HRM strategies that are aligned to the business; the identification and assessment of HR risks of the impending M&A transaction; and management integration upon the conclusion of the deal.

Key words: due diligence, state-owned enterprise, strategic intent, greenfield, negotiations, integration

M&A from a HRM perspective

M&A activities are becoming more sophisticated and commonplace in Asia. For China, the developments of capital and securities markets, banking reforms and the adoption of international financial and accounting standards to the market economy system attract massive direct foreign investment into the inner cities and the special administrative regions (Taylor, 2002). Since 1978, foreign multinational corporations (MNCs) have capitalised on the enormous potential of the domestic market by investing in Chinese businesses (Shenkar, 2005). Xiao and Zhang (2005) argue that 'the M&A market, where China is now ranked as the leader in the Asia Pacific Region, is increasingly becoming a focal point on the global scene'. As the Chinese economy grew rapidly, strategic foreign investment policies and stringent regulations were progressively introduced, reviewed and updated to reflect market conditions (Davies, 2003). For example, restrictions were placed to prevent foreign investors from dominating key domestic industries (Swanston, 2006) and investments were being directed to rural areas of China to rejuvenate old-economy sectors with newer technologies. In a rush to tap into the huge domestic market, direct foreign investments to China appear to have been generated rather hastily under premature guidelines and/or primitive legal protection. As a consequence, some of its assets arguably may be priced below market valuation and sold hurriedly to foreign investors. In addition, large scale privatisation, particularly of SOEs, was deemed necessary 'to fund a ballooning social security deficit' (Chen, 2006).

Reforming SOEs has since become one of the most important objectives for the Chinese government. Bureaucratically-led SOEs are continually being reorganised into corporations with functioning boards of directors and stakeholder ownership. With the restructuring of SOEs, millions of workers in the urban areas were laid off, causing grave social discontent amongst their people. For Tong (2007), 'the decades-long government efforts of grappling with the SOEs reform problem have produced many encouraging results though many problems remain unresolved'. Tong (2007) adds that 'in 2005, for example, while stated-owned and state-controlled enterprises accounted for 11 per cent of all above-scale industrial establishments, 21 per cent of all loss-making enterprises were SOEs or state-controlled'.

Human resource due diligence

Due diligence may be defined as a comprehensive assessment of a business undertaken by or on behalf of a prospective investor to establish the exact scope of current assets and liabilities, and to evaluate future commercial potential. The purpose of conducting due diligence is to uncover potential issues and unseen business risks by taking into account the legal, financial and human resource challenges. Specifically, the human resource management due diligence process seeks to establish employment-related costs in an organisation, especially its unseen costs. This is pertinent for the Chinese SOEs as employment-related costs are usually unsaid, unseen or left unnoticed, and therefore not uncovered. The Chinese are accustomed to rigid secrecy policies and may be reluctant to volunteer information and therefore be perceived as uncooperative in disclosing their records (Peng, 2006). In addition, organisation policies and routines are often unavailable, or unreliable if made available. It is common knowledge that the Chinese may maintain discrete sets of books to satisfy different stakeholders, thereby creating doubt among foreign investors. For Ho and Koh (2006), the perceptions of the Chinese as uncooperative and difficult to convince may be attributed to the fact that foreign investors are unfamiliar with traditional Chinese business practices.

Human resource management practitioners are playing a more strategic role in mergers and acquisitions (Lin et al., 2006; Aguliera et al., 2004). While research has been undertaken to 'make sense' of HRM in China, as cited in the *International Journal of Human Resource Management*, Vol. 20, No. 11, November 2009, there has been little published work on the people aspects of due diligence of M&A in the Chinese context. Human resource management due diligence processes are often overlooked, and the people issues (Kay et al., 2002; Corwin et al., 1991) are examined only after M&A deals are concluded. An acquiring organisation, Harding and Rouse (2007) comment, begins with the strategic intent of the acquisition. An understanding of the purpose of the acquisition is predicated on the equity participation of foreign investors in Chinese state-owned enterprises. Translating strategic intent and equity participation of foreign and Chinese state-owned investors into human resource management challenges, the scenario planning of HRM in mergers and acquisitions includes:

- A single business entity is created when a foreign investor injects capital into an existing business unit of a state-owned enterprise.

- A new joint venture company is created from a merger of the business unit of the foreign investor and the business unit of the state-owned enterprise.

- A two-phase merger process: the first being when a joint venture company is created when the foreign investor injects capital and the state-owned enterprise injects assets into the venture. In phase two, upon successful management of the JV from the Chinese perspective, the foreign investor continues to inject capital into the joint venture and the state-owned enterprise injects additional assets and people into the newly formed joint venture company.

- The state-owned enterprise injects its physical assets and seconds its employees to the newly formed joint venture company for a fixed term whilst the foreign investor injects capital.

Based on equity participation of stakeholders and the motives of M&A, different human resource management challenges are invoked. For a foreign investor injecting capital into an existing business unit of a state-owned enterprise to form a single entity, a potential challenge is in its human resource staffing level, which is likely to be disproportionately higher. In the case of a direct merger of the business unit of the foreign investor and that of the state-owned enterprise, the consolidation of sets of employment terms and conditions, employee compensation and benefit of the separate entities may be extremely difficult and costly.

Role and activities of HR due diligence by phase

In an HR due diligence process, the activities may be grouped into three main phases: the upstream phase, the midstream phase and the downstream phase. To achieve successful implementation of the phases, there are distinct HR activities in each phase that warrant careful planning and close attention. The real-life exposure of one of the authors to M&A deals in China confirmed that the HR function has a significant role in brownfield projects, particularly on the transfer of employees from a Chinese entity to either a joint venture (JV) or a wholly foreign-owned enterprise. There appears to be a link between the role of HR and the complexity of the organisation, in terms of its size and structure: the larger headcount and complexity of the organisation increases the role of the HR function. It is not a matter that a higher headcount implies higher costs per employee, but fundamentally, the number of employees and its organisation structure will invariably lead to huge challenges on the integration of the business units at a later stage. In the case of a greenfield project, the absence of the people issue in itself will relieve the management of a plethora of HR related issues and risks. In an acquisition where the company is either a wholly-owned foreign enterprise or a majority-controlled enterprise of the foreign partner, the decision making process is relatively straightforward, and issues may be expeditiously dealt with.

The upstream phase

Three main activities in an upstream phase are the identification of the M&A target; the initial preparation of a potential M&A transaction; and the adoption of an appropriate HR strategy to achieve successful completion of the transaction.

Identification of M&A target

Notwithstanding the fact that M&A is very much a business-driven activity, it is important that the HR function is made aware of and participates actively in a potential M&A discussion. Questions that are fundamental to the discussion include:

- What, and how much, value can the HR function add?
- Is the transaction a merger or an acquisition?
- How will the newly merged or acquired company be structured as a part of a national organisation, or otherwise?

The key point to emphasise is that preparations should commence as early as possible. Early preparation helps HR focus on its key objectives (which are aligned to the business objectives), which will invariably affect the appropriate HR strategy to be employed at a later stage. It is important to note that once this strategy is determined, discussion continues to evolve around the dynamics of negotiation. The progress of the due diligence discussion and the negotiations may affect the strategy that was determined at initial preparation. A certain degree of flexibility is required as business considerations may cause problems during HR Due Diligence strategy making. The formulation of relevant HR strategy is explained in detail in the subsequent chapters.

At the very core of HR understanding are business challenges identified as deal makers or deal breakers. For a challenge to be considered as either a deal maker or a deal breaker, it must be overriding when measured against all other factors, regardless of the relative importance of the given factor attributed to the department or corporate function. What this amounts to is that HR issues or factors or risks will always be subservient to business considerations. This does not imply that HR issues may be dispensed with or ignored, but they may usually be deferred to a later stage of discussion. In several instances, HR issues may become useful for subsequent business Due Diligence discussion as a negotiation trade-off when attempting to secure a deal-breaking factor. While the HR issue may not always be discussed at HR group negotiation level, those issues may be escalated at a business and perhaps at a higher level to aid strategic negotiations in deal-making.

The first thing in an identification of M&A targets is to understand what the business objectives are which lead to the identification of such targets for an M&A transaction. At the start of an information gathering stage, it is good to be made aware of the target company, where it is located, the nature of its business, its own business strategy going forward, and the broad background of the target company (is it part of a group, when was it founded and what is its positioning or standing within the locality?). These are important items of information to gather as they are potentially HR risk factors. A clear awareness of all these, even on a preliminary basis, goes some way towards framing the specific risks to be assessed when one gets to the phase of HR risk assessment.

The initial preparation

When making initial preparation, it is important to determine whether one already has operating units in the vicinity of the target company or in a neighbouring city which is in close proximity. The purpose of this study is to verify what the operational impacts are in the event that the M&A deal should follow through. If it is a merger deal, it is imperative to have a clear indication as to whether the intent is for both Chinese and foreign parties to inject existing assets, people or capital into the JV, and which party (Chinese or foreign) has management control of the newly formed JV company. The way the JV is structured has a profound impact on HR. Whether the foreign party pumps in only capital and/or assets with or without people brings to the fore entirely different HR considerations. If people are injected into the JV by both parties, HR would have to deal with the issue of integrating two sets of employees. This would include harmonising the different sets of terms and conditions of employment, particularly compensation and employee benefits to be made relevant to the newly formed JV company. Besides having to manage the assimilation of employment terms and conditions, there may be the additional challenge of excess headcount arising from integrating the two business units into a single entity. The bigger challenge that will surface subsequently will be the business unit with the excess headcount. Even if the decision taken to integrate is made by both original business units, the criterion to adopt must be perceived and seen by both business units to be fair and equitable, and its ultimate success can only be measured by the general acceptance of the combined workforce. Even in an acquisition deal, the consideration for HR is similar, except that one does not need to deal with the Chinese partner in terms of communication and gaining support as leverage towards the smoother resolution of problem areas. Issues of integrating two sets of employees from two business units, if such is the business intent, remain largely the same from an HR perspective.

Hence, an awareness of the background of the Chinese party is vital. The following questions are pertinent:

- Is it a state-owned set-up or is it privately owned? If it is a state-owned entity, where is this particular business unit placed in the overall organisation structure of the group or conglomerate?

- What is the significance of this business to the local community (be it at district, city or provincial level) in terms of its contribution to its GDP, employment impact and seniority of its management personnel vis-à-vis local government officials?

- Is the nature of the industry that this entity is engaged in considered to be part of the national key industries grouping?

These questions will highlight the prominence of being attached to this business unit. Being in the limelight can be a disadvantage. On the one hand, being prominent will mean that problems will likely get a quick hearing. At the same time, problems, once they have surfaced, will also mean public scrutiny and close official monitoring. In other words, such entities are particularly media-sensitive and employees are likely to be wise to this perspective as well.

Since HR as a profession is primarily people-focused, it is imperative that headcount be an area of concern. Once the staffing level of this business is known, the next thing to do is to make a preliminary comparison against one's own best-practice businesses and acquire a sense of how this target unit would rank, assuming that detailed information is available. This will provide an indication to any potential issue of over-staffing.

Determining the appropriate HR strategy to adopt

The appropriate HR strategy for an M&A transaction is predicated upon the business objectives for the given merger or acquisition transaction. At the forefront is the fundamental question as to whether the potential deal is a merger or an acquisition. Is this a greenfield or a brownfield project? If the merger is for a greenfield project, HR should know the equity participation and the rights and responsibilities to management control. The complexity and depth of the issues will come on-stream when the project entails either a merger or acquisition of a brownfield nature. HR due diligence should not be taken to be a stand-alone study, which commences and ends with the present merger or acquisition project. A strategically conceived M&A HR due diligence should look beyond the present circumstances into the future. What does this signify? For a start, consideration should be focused on whether the business intends to bring additional assets into the M&A after a specified period of time. If the answer is 'yes', what form will this be likely to take? Questions as to whether both parties are expected to inject equivalent physical assets and people into the JV should be addressed. If there is a likelihood of additional people being brought into the merger transaction at a later stage, HR should factor the additional headcount into the current strategy.

The midstream phase

There are four main stages in the midstream phase of the due diligence process. These are:

- Identify HR-related risks.
- Conduct HR due diligence.
- Negotiations.
- Draft HR paragraph for M&A agreement.

Identifying HR-related risks

HR-related risks can be grouped into three broad areas. These are:

- management related
- cost related
- behaviour related.

Under each of these categories, there are individual risk items to examine in detail for an assessment exercise to be conducted. The purpose of carrying out such an assessment is to determine which specific items are rated as being of high risk. Risk assessments in the context of HR due diligence may be interpreted at two levels: identification, and implementation stages.

At the identification level, a high risk rating would imply that the probability of the risk occurring is high and the impact on the business when the risk arises is also high. At the implementation level, this same risk may carry a high degree of difficulty in being managed and the time taken to control the risks is lengthy. Those which are thus rated as high risks require mitigation plans to be put in place to address each of them as and when any of these identified risks arise.

Conducting HR due diligence

This is an activity where the entire due diligence team, including the human resource members, will conduct on-site studies, and will check, verify and analyse all essential information. This is also an opportunity to build a relationship and networking with the Chinese partners. A comprehensive checklist of information to gather, usually prepared at the risk identification stage if not earlier, will be extremely useful. As a word of advice, what is being asked may not necessarily be what is being understood by the Chinese. As an example, if one were to ask for information pertaining to gross salary, the interpretation of gross salary in the Chinese context will be very different from the Westernised idea of what constitutes gross salary. More importantly, the information that we seek from the Chinese counterpart is not usually what we may expect as the working definitions differ. Hence, no party can be adjudged to be incorrect about the accuracy or adequacy of data or information provided. The explanation stems invariably from the fact that both parties are talking tangentially even though they are referring to the same subject matter. It takes many face to face meetings to forge a shared meaning and understanding between team members.

Another ground rule to establish is the authenticity and authoritativeness of information provided. This issue of information takes on these aspects:

- To avoid disputes arising from unofficial information being given, all information should preferably stem from a single source.
- Preferably, the information provided should be appropriately endorsed and signed by the designated authority to signify its authenticity and the official status of the signatories.

- It must be possible to check the validity of information after the JV has been formed.

For these points to be accepted and enforceable, an understanding between the parties must be put in place. This understanding must include the following:

- identification of a central source for the request and supply of all information;
- definition of the penalty to be applied where inaccuracy or inadequacy of information leads to a significant increase in costs;
- definitions of the conditions under which information is classified as official; e.g. it must be signed and authenticated by the designated authority.

Negotiations

Rules of engagement should be agreed and observed before the parties commence negotiations. The first is the question of the taking of minutes of meetings. Which party is responsible for this? How should the minutes be made official? In what language should these minutes be taken? In the event that a given point of negotiation has reached amicable conclusion, how will this be formalised?

There are two structured ways of doing this. The first method is to incorporate the agreement into the minutes of the meeting and the other is to have it formalised by way of all parties signing the agreement. The signature method may be more systematic as it precludes the need to locate all these points of discussion amongst the minutes, which may be voluminous, depending on how prolonged the negotiations turn out to be.

Yet another point of consideration is the venue for the negotiations. Going for a neutral location brings into contention the issue of costs.

It is advisable to adopt a suitable HR strategy before entering into negotiations. What is suitable as an HR strategy very much depends on the nature of the equity participation in the merger or acquisition.

Drafting the HR paragraph for an M&A agreement

The drafting on the HR portion of the agreement would normally be the responsibility of the legal team. However, there are selected HR terms that can be unique or specific to HR. Efforts must be directed to ensure that HR specific terms are correctly captured and reflect the exact essence and nuances.

In addition, attention should be focused on the area of translation. It is essential for foreign executives to be aware that M&A agreements are necessarily in Hanyu, which is the version to rely on to settle disputes, notwithstanding the fact that the agreement may be drafted in other languages also. That HR has an important role to contribute to the drafting of the HR portion of the M&A agreement to ensure that agreements are not lost in translation. Besides ensuring that nuances and HR specialist terms are appropriately captured, the other aspect to carefully guard against is that areas which are to be omitted from the mainstream agreement be recorded elsewhere and these documents are deemed legal in the law of the land.

The downstream phase

- Formation of the management team
- Handing/taking over administration
- Integration: organisation, benefits structure and culture/ values

Formation of the management team

As one nears the conclusion of the negotiations process, it also marks the stage where the foreign party should finalise the people who will be assigned to manage the newly acquired enterprise or newly established joint venture. Besides the appointment of the business unit general manager, there are those who report directly to the manager. The fundamental question is whether to appoint expatriates to these positions (which had been agreed to be held by the foreign party appointee). The underlying point of contention is that of costs, which are not merely remuneration-related but other expatriation items such as housing, children's education, transport-related (e.g. provision of a driver), tax-related (e.g. arising out of tax equalisation or protection), spouse assistance, etc. This issue of financial costs has to be balanced against non-financial aspects like cultural alignment, regional/global networking, way of working, language proficiency and competencies fit. Moreover, there is also the issue of the Chinese partner's concurrence with the appointment of an expatriate to address, if this is a joint venture. These issues take on greater significance when one enters the phase of integrating the business entity into the entire web of the group structure. Against this backdrop lies the all-important element of risks entailed. Do these considerations stand up to scrutiny when one brings in the factors of standards and governance? Frequently, these are the least stress-tested issues. It is not uncommon to see overwhelming reliance on technical competencies. As long as the person possesses the capabilities to meet the requirements the job dictates, it will suffice. The processes and behavioural aspects are largely overlooked. Our experience tells us that failure will likely stem from these rather than from the hard technical factors.

Handing/taking over administration

Upon the signing of the M&A agreement and with consent being reached on a mutually suitable date for handing/taking over of the business, plans must be made to ensure that this is carried out smoothly without unnecessary disputes. One way of preventing disputes from arising is to have a plan that is discussed and agreed between both parties. Such a plan will include the scope of the handing/taking over exercise, persons assigned to deal with respective tasks and sub-tasks, methods of dealing with outstanding items (i.e. those items which are either incomplete or missing), damages and inaccuracies (i.e. those items or information which purportedly were either over- or understated). For this reason alone, it is imperative that close attention be paid and an understanding be reached during the negotiations phase to deal with the following:

- outstanding items that are uncovered
- damages
- inaccuracies.

What is the desired outcome in each of these situations?

Even before the advent of negotiations, preparations outlining the scope of the takeover should have been made. This will provide the platform from which issues are to be raised and grappled with when negotiations get underway.

Integration: organisation, benefits structure and culture/values

The completion of the handing/taking over exercise marks the beginning of a new chapter for all concerned; a new board, new management team and transferred employees (who can be described as 'existing' and not new). The first challenge facing them will be how the business entity is to be integrated into the group business. This challenge can be broadly classified into three dimensions: namely, the organisational structure, the employment benefits and the organisational culture to be assimilated. Each of these dimensions takes on a different complexion and calls for a varied strategy in its treatment. The one common thread that runs through all three is the question of timing. Within what timeline should each of these be implemented? Putting any one on the back burner may mean that old and bad habits will remain entrenched and – worse still – be seen as institutionalised and accepted as a way of work life. At the same time, doing one too many things concurrently will mean an overload of initiatives.

4

Conducting HR due diligence

Abstract: The differences between the Chinese ways of doing things as measured against Westernised work practice may be leveraged and harmonised by adopting a standardised framework whenever Human Resource Due Diligence interventions are undertaken. Almost every situation or critical factor formulated within the framework from inside-out is examined in sufficient details to uncover HR risks that would otherwise be left unseen. In most instances, the critical factors revolve around people management and people-related costs issues.

Key words: inside-out, risks, people-related costs, internal controls, unknowing, due diligence framework, mitigation plans

The strategic objectives

In the corporate world, where organisational growth and profitability are paramount, the ultimate performance of leaders and their respective organisational functions is measured and evaluated against a set of targets commonly known as key performance indicators. Embedded in each indicator are the critical success factors, whose neglect will probably lead to failures in individual and organisational performance. The underlying principle to the key performance indicators is its strategic objectives. For the purpose of conducting HR due diligence, the basic requirement is similar: to determine the primary objectives. The objectives will determine the appropriate tone and focus at each phase of the due diligence process.

In the case of a financial due diligence, the main focus is on the valuation of the entire assets and liabilities of the target for merger and acquisition. This can be described as looking at the current state of affairs to arrive at a fair value to be agreed by buyer and seller. However, in the case of the human resource function, the costs and its impact take effect only after the M&A deal is concluded, that is, upon the taking over of the merged business. While the financial evaluation determines the front-end sunk-in investment outlay, the human resource portion examines the back-end operational costs of business. Therefore, the main objective for the conduct of an HR due diligence revolves around knowing the full extent of its back-end operational costs and non-financial issues: an impact on costs or unresolved human resource issues with a future financial burden. Any omission of such costs or issues will ultimately result in an erosion of its operating profits.

The first objective of due diligence is to 'uncover the unseen costs'. Although this may appear obvious, the first thing that one examines will be human resource related costs. Obvious as it may seem or sound, it is not an overstatement that an inexperienced, unexposed and unknowing china practitioner is likely to examine only the books and reports of the target business unit. It is likely that they will not look beyond these books and reports; the reason is simply lack of familiarity. The unseen cost of human resource is unseen only because one does not know where to look. It is simply a question of being familiar with the way the Chinese go about dealing with things, and the consequences. Unfortunately, it can be construed by the non-Chinese as the deliberate intent of the Chinese to mislead or hide information from view.

The second objective is to understand the organisational strengths and shortcomings of the target business unit. It involves the study of the entire human resource operating systems; policies and procedures; and processes and practices that are in place. The purpose is to identify those to retain, and to segregate those that require rectification or updating. Systems, procedural, policy or process weaknesses can result in undesirable work habits and practices. An example is an instance of a deeply entrenched but unstated practice or an inadequately worded claims policy in conducting the business. The basic questions that a Westernised, trained internal control executive would focus on are as follows:

- What are the items which qualify for claims?
- What is the monetary limit of such claims for each item?
- Are the monetary limits determined by the seniority of the position holder?
- What is the basis for approving claims in the case of an unstated practice?

There is a tendency for the Chinese to think that what is not explicitly prohibited is tacitly permitted. Often, a Chinese may argue a case by stating that the policy does not explicitly preclude his conduct. From this simple example, one can thus see that an organisational analysis of claims in itself will draw out potential challenges that one needs to keep in mind before the handing and taking over of the management of the business.

The third objective is to uncover people-related issues which may potentially pose problems to subsequent integration after the management of the business unit is handed over. Uncovering the people-related challenges at the outset may facilitate a smooth and meticulous management integration of the business, precluding people-related issues from arising in the early stages of taking over the business. In so doing, it will free the management team from having to expend time and effort in dealing with post-merger issues. Thereafter, the integration team can focus on delivering their strategies and business performance indicators. This stage is characterised by the identification of human resource risks, assessing the probability and impact of each risk. If the assessment reveals a rating of a risk factor denoting both a high degree of probability and impact, then it is imperative that these factors be selected for further deliberation.

Once the people-related issues and risks are uncovered, the next objective is to put in place mitigation plans to address these high-risk issues. For mitigation plans to be optimally effective, they must address two considerations; manageability and timeliness. Manageability refers to the ease of managing the issue in the event that it should arise, and timeliness refers to how quickly the adopted solution can be implemented. It will be of little use if the issue can be easily managed but the time needed to put it in place is unacceptably long.

Finally, thought must be given to the all-important consideration of whether the targeted organisation has the relevant personnel resources with the right balance of know-how, cultural fit and competencies to adequately manage the issues identified. A proven performance record in the home country may not be adequate for a leadership position in the newly acquired turf of a host country. Cultural nuances can be overwhelmingly difficult to overcome.

The need for a due diligence that spans the human resource dimension, especially in China, cannot be overstated. It must be done with sufficient rigour and not simply perfunctory, as oversights or mistakes, regardless of intention, can cost the company dearly.

Perspectives in HR due diligence

Scholars and practitioners have written about mergers and acquisitions globally, and specifically on China. The challenge is whether there is anything of value to contribute to the body of knowledge that scholars and practitioners would benefit from. In recent decades, China's breakneck economic development coupled with unprecedented foreign direct investments inflow has been widely publicised. In addition, China as a huge, heterogeneous and complex country is well documented. In an article on 'The Nine Nations of China', Patrick Chovanec, an Associate Professor at Beijing's Tsinghua School of Economics and Management, observed that, 'We tend to imagine China as a monolith. The truth is far more interesting. China is a mosaic of several distinct regions, each with its own resources, dynamics and historical character.' In the work of John and Doris Naisbitt, on 'China's Megatrends', China is viewed from an 'outside-in or inside-out' perspective. Adopting an outside-in approach would be to look at China through a pair of Western glasses with assumptions that are obtained from experiences derived from the Western economies. With an inside-out approach, the view is to 'look at China as the Chinese look at their country; be open to its shortcomings, but [. . .] not judge China by our own values and standards'. Does an inside-out view of China offer valuable lessons to draw on as the task of conducting a due diligence is measured against a given target? As Cambridge Professor Joseph Needham observed, the Chinese had a 'different way of doing things' that is unaffected by others from the outside world; the Naisbitts are advocating that one should rely on viewing things through the eyes of the Chinese. Leveraging on the idea, it is useful to substitute China with Chinese industry and the country with the company and its systems and processes. The outcome is to adopt a detached look at Chinese industries in the same manner that mainland Chinese would look at their own companies. Notwithstanding the comments by the Naisbitts not to judge, the objectives for the conduct of an HR due diligence dictate the awareness of the differences between the Chinese way or standards as measured against a commonly used best-practice yardstick or an internal measurement standard. Such differences may pose as hazards or risks. The gap may be bridged by formulating a framework which interested parties can rely on when conducting an HR due diligence exercise. This framework needs to satisfy those key factors that commonly impact any due diligence efforts that corporations undertake through the lens of human resource management. In addition, the need to examine every situation or critical factor inside-out is advocated. Broadly, these factors would revolve around people management issues and people-related costs issues. The two issues are exceedingly broad and require an in-depth examination. From an initial conceptualisation, a four-step methodology is proposed. The steps translate into organisational, legal, and internal controls and costs.

Framing all the factors into these four perspectives provides the methodical framework to examine potential implications exhaustively in a structured and detailed manner. Within an organisational perspective, the areas to be investigated thoroughly are:

- organisational structure
- role and authority of the party secretary
- role of the trade union
- superfluous departments

- manning levels
- Xin Gang (下 岗) or Nei Tui (內 退) employees
- scrutiny of job descriptions
- systems integrity and continuity
- security.

Having examined the organisation-related issues, the legal-related issues are reviewed. These include:

- scrutiny of employment contracts
- scrutiny of HR policies, systems and processes
- extraneous contractual obligations
- scrutiny of employee handbook and HR manual
- outstanding payments.

Once the organisational and legal perspectives have been adequately dealt with, internal controls are studied. The controls include:

- internal control procedures
- authorisation policy
- HR-related claims procedures
- company chop (or seal)
- leave administration
- work attendance
- disciplinary procedures and cases
- performance management.

To complete the HR due diligence, the focus turns to costs that incorporate:

- employment costs and payroll control
- benefits administration

- compensation management/scrutiny of compensation and benefits policy
- training costs
- administration processes and procedures
- shared services and facilities.

The organisational perspective

Organisational structure

One of the very first things to examine is the organisational structure. It is not surprising, in certain instances, that those documents are not available. In such a situation, one can only ask for the material to be drawn up, explained and rationalised. An organisational chart in itself may only provide an impression of the way the functions are structured and differentiated. Invariably, probing questions need to be raised to obtain a deeper insight into how roles and responsibilities are segregated and defined. Any unclear segregation or ill-defined roles could give rise to only two possibilities. On one hand, there may be areas which are constantly ignored or not attended to because either parties or sections do not wish to handle the task or issues. On the other, there may be constant friction or disputes which will ultimately affect collaboration and cohesiveness. Regardless, it remains an issue for management.

It is critical not just to examine the way the target business unit is organised into the various departments or functions, but to probe deeply to the last position. Probing the organisational levels to the final details may reveal indicators that point to areas of concern. Is the structure an unwieldy one? Are there functions or sections which appear unaligned to the core business? Are there any departments which show overstaffing compared to all other departments?

As soon as the structure and the departmental staffing statistics are analysed, the next item to be scrutinised is the first line management level and the management team. Individual profiles of the managers and the management teams should be reviewed to obtain a good grasp of their individual background, work exposure and career growth. In the case of the management team, it is important to determine if there are any members who do not hold the position of departmental head. If such instances do occur, an investigation must be carried out to determine the rationale for such practice. This could possibly point to sensitivity of a non-business nature, which may warrant delicate handling at some point in the future.

In a joint venture situation, the final decision on the choice of heads of respective departments is subject to negotiations between the two parties involved. In all likelihood, the negotiations will revolve around having an equal (if the number of departments is even) or near-equal split (if the number is odd). It is equally likely that both parties desire to have the right to select what is perceived to be the 'controlling' departments, i.e. the line departments which have a direct control over the running of the business. If, for instance, the business unit is engaged in manufacturing, then both parties would desire to have the right to appoint the operations and finance portfolios. Ultimately, it boils down to what is finally agreed upon. The delicate part of this particular point relates to the legal relationship between the respective nominee and the joint venture partners. For example, if the finance manager is to be nominated by the foreign party by mutual agreement, then the question will arise as to whether he will be transferred from the foreign company to the newly formed joint venture. The corollary would be the terms and conditions of employment in the joint venture arrangement. The likelihood that the salary and benefits in the wholly foreign-owned enterprise are significantly higher than those of the SOE (assuming that the Chinese partner is such an entity) is great. There are several plausible alternatives in dealing with this issue.

1. Integrate the terms and conditions for all joint venture departmental heads to be in line with this particular nominee. This carries a costs implication that one needs to look into, provided the Chinese partner concurs with this action.

2. Treat all departmental heads as a secondment from the respective partner to the joint venture. In other words, all departmental heads are not employees of the joint venture but remain as employees of their respective parent companies. There are two consequences to grapple with. The first is the issue of charging the costs of the respective secondees. As the ones from the foreign company carry higher costs, will the Chinese party be amenable to such a move? The second entails an issue of loyalty to the parent organisation.

3. For this option, the terms and conditions of the respective secondees are left intact and all the nominees from both sides are transferred to the joint venture on an 'as is' basis. This option is certainly not without its attendant issues. The more immediate issue that will arise will be one of subsequent awareness on the part of the nominees from the Chinese SOE, which will translate into perceived unfair treatment and discontent. What can make matters worse is that this ill-feeling will cascade downwards to the general workforce.

4. Another alternative is for the nominees to be attached to the joint venture on a loan basis. What this means is that

the nominees remain on the payroll of their parent company and their respective costs are charged to the JV on a fixed management fee, the quantum of which is to be agreed between the two parties. Whatever difference arises between the actual costs and the agreed management fees will be borne by the party concerned.

5. The final option is to have all the nominees for the various departmental head roles filled by managers from the Chinese SOE. This is predicated on the assumption that the foreign partner will find that all of their personal profiles have a close fit to the prerequisites that the various roles demand. This would be an ideal situation that will circumvent the various issues which we have elaborated upon.

To add to the complication, the nominee may be an expatriate employee. The aggregated costs of the expatriate employee (taking into account all overseas assignment benefits such as housing, children's education, tax equalisation or protection benefits, etc.) are significantly higher than those of local Chinese employees. Another area of complexity is the principle of job rotation of nominees, which will arise in the event that the agreement that was reached in the course of negotiations is for each party to the joint venture to make nominations to the desired departmental head positions for a fixed tenure of office, after which it will rotate to the other party. Such an arrangement is likely to have two adverse effects. First, it can create disruption to management on each occasion when a rotation is due to take effect. Secondly, one cannot rule out the possibility that the Chinese party will ask for an assistant manager to be appointed for every department so that the main nominee takes the head role whilst the secondary nominee assumes the assistant role. This will then escalate overall employment costs for the joint venture.

Role and authority of the party secretary

In pre-reform days when China was a highly centralised planned economy, the government and corporate functions were not distinct and separate. They were, in fact, closely intertwined. As all businesses were virtually owned and managed by the government, they lacked the rights and vitality of an independently-run entity. As owners, the government made all the decisions and the corporate managers were only expected to execute those decisions. Internal governance was achieved through a structure of checks and balances embedded within a three-power centre. These power centres comprise the following:

1. corporate directors or managers who are primarily responsible for the daily production and management

2. the secretary of the Communist Party Committee, who is responsible for personnel and party affairs as well as the supervision of the enterprise operations

3. workers' council.

The party secretary and workers' council assume the joint role of acting as the check and balance against the power and influence of the enterprise managers. Since the party secretary has the responsibility to supervise the enterprise operations, it would imply that s/he certainly wields considerable influence over the way in which the business is managed. What is intriguing is the fact that there are occasions when the factory director and the party secretary are one and the same person. Without a segregation of roles, the supervisory responsibility is eroded or removed. Even with a clear segregation of roles between the position of the factory director and that of the party secretary, the fact that there is an air of collaboration between the two position-holders need not mean that it is a healthy indicator for the business.

In fact, there have been cases of meeting or convergence of personal interests which led to collusion and pursuit of personal gains at the expense of the enterprise. These are potential hazards that one should keep a keen lookout for. In a research piece on 'Party Control in China's Listed Firms', Wei Yu of the Shanghai Institute of Foreign Trade comments that 'the existence of a party secretary is negatively associated with a firm's performance, but only in SOEs. Non-state firms with a party secretary are more likely to have senior managers with political connections, but less professionalism'.

Role of the trade union

Currently, there is only one national trade union in the People's Republic of China, and that is the All-China Federation of Trade Unions (ACFTU). The ACFTU is divided into 31 regional federations and 10 national industrial unions, representing workers in the Railway; Agriculture, Forestry and Water Conservancy; Aviation; Banking; Defence, Postal and Telecommunications; Education, Scientific, Cultural, Medical and Sports; Energy and Chemical; Financial, Communications, Light Industry, Textile and Tobacco; Machinery, Metallurgical and Building Materials; and Seamen and Construction Industries. Although it was founded as long ago as 1 May 1925, it has nevertheless undergone profound changes, including its dissolution during the Cultural Revolution of 1966–76. It was only in the 1990s that a law was promulgated to regulate the trade union in China. As recently as 2008, a new labour law made it compulsory for all companies, including wholly foreign-owned ones, to form branch unions that are sanctioned by the ACFTU. Competing unions are illegal in China. However, it is appropriate for any industrial relations practitioners in China to take note that the International

Confederation of Free Trade Unions (ICFTU) views the ACFTU as not being an independent trade union as it does not represent workers' rights. How did such a stance come about over the years that the trade union has existed in China? What does the representation of defence of workers' rights amount to?

Traditionally, the trade union in China plays a role which is vastly different from the adversarial and collective bargaining relationship that is prevalent in the Westernised economies. In China, the trade union assumes the role of a welfare organisation without any collective bargaining function. The union is committed to 'fighting for' rather than 'fighting to better' the rights and benefits of its worker members. It organises activities for the members and their families, such as outings, company dinners and hospital visits during periods of hospitalisation as well as providing help with wedding and funeral arrangements. This does not in any way suggest that the traditional trade union in China does not get embroiled in fighting for the rights or benefits of workers. For example, in the case of a termination of a worker's contract of employment, then the union will likely look into the case to ensure that there has been fair play and justification in the termination decision. Having determined fair play, the union will also fight to ensure that the worker gets the best compensation from the termination. If one were to ask veteran trade union leaders represented at the company level whether the unions fight for and defend workers' rights in China, one will certainly draw a ferocious defence that the unions in China exist to represent workers' rights and illustrations will pour forth to justify such a view. Why then is there such a divergence in viewpoints between what the Western unions uphold versus that of the Chinese union leaders, no matter at which level this question is posed? The issue lies in the fact that the concept of industrial relations and collective bargaining is alien to the trade union movement in China but this is about to change. In 1998, China passed the Declaration on Fundamental Principles and Rights at Work and embodied in these rights is collective bargaining.

This scenario from a welfare based role is therefore heading towards a tumultuous change. International organisations, including the Geneva-based International Labour Organization, are pressurising China to adopt collective bargaining as a fundamental tool for the trade union movement to take root. China appears to be responding with caution but certainly moving gradually towards developing such a characteristic in its industrial relations scene. In recent years, collective agreements have been introduced into some companies, especially in the cities of Beijing and Shanghai. Amongst the most prominent cases to be widely publicised is the news release in July 2008 that the US supermarket chain Walmart signed collective agreements in two provinces. This piece of information is interesting as Walmart is known to exit marketplaces rather than deal with trade unions. And yet in China, they seemed to have yielded. Is there anything beneath the surface that more than meets the eye? Concept is one thing and translating it into reality is something else entirely. The acid test is when collective agreements incorporating features of freely negotiated employment benefits are commonly made available across industries. This will happen when increasing numbers of China's local trade union leaders at the provincial, district and industry levels become familiar with and competent in the art of industrial relations. The Westernised economies need to exercise patience as the industrial relations scene is being transformed into a market-driven workplace. Time is certainly needed to develop industrial relations competencies of the branch leaders in the art of industrial relations.

Superfluous departments

For the purpose of this chapter, 'superfluous' departments are those departments which either have no direct relevance to the business or are excessive to the organisational needs of the predator entity. On paper, for anyone to claim that any given department of an operating unit has no relevance to the business would certainly appear to be an illogical comment. In the first place, it does not make sense for anyone even to imagine that a department that is lodged within an industrial or commercial organisation can be described as having no relevance to its business. Why should the entity bear the operating costs of a department that is not making any contribution to its business efforts? There are two possible explanations for this seemingly illogical feature. First, this department could have been transplanted into this target business entity when the decision was taken to spin it off through a merger or a divestment. The second explanation is that the group is looking at diversifying into a new business sector and is using this particular target M&A entity to bear its start-up costs. Alternatively, the group comprises a complex web of companies with different shareholding structures. In such a case, the objective for doing so is to transfer the costs burden to the entity where the shareholding interests are relatively low as compared to the other entities within the group. Whatever the reasons, it nevertheless points to one plausible conclusion: the practice is ethically questionable or shows a lack of integrity. Therefore, the leader responsible for conducting the HR Due Diligence has the key responsibility to study the organisational structure of the target company in detail to ensure that any superfluous activities are removed.

It is also possible that a 'superfluous' department that does not have any business fit with the overall business plan of the predator company does not behave ethically, or lacks integrity. In such a situation, this issue of a 'superfluous' department must be raised at the outset of the M&A exercise with the Chinese party. If there is no alignment of the department with the business, it is likely that the Chinese will be amenable to have the 'superfluous' department and all employees excluded from the headcount of the business unit being targeted for M&A.

Assembling the management team

In a merger or acquisition situation, it is never too early to assemble a management team as soon as the process of management handing/taking over commences. In making this assessment, the underlying issue to contend with is the cultural values of every manager. Are their cultural values tangential with the organisation values that are strictly upheld by the foreign party? Will expatriate managers be brought in to bridge the transition, considering the fact that expatriate costs are significantly higher than a grossed-up local managerial cost? If the final decision is that an expatriate manager must be assigned to bridge the cultural values or expertise gap, then an analysis needs to be done to determine the length of time that is required to localise the position.

Manning levels

A singular feature that characterises SOEs from a human resource standpoint is the excessive staffing level. In Philip Lewis's research on 'New China – Old Ways' of May 2002, he comments 'under the iron-rice bowl system, "featherbedding" existed where enterprises were overstaffed with a subsequent observation that the Industrial and

Commercial Bank of China was probably ten times over-resourced'. Perhaps a manning level of a multiple of ten times may appear far-fetched and grossly excessive. From the field experience of the author working in China for more than a decade, a multiple of 3.5 to 5 times is a common benchmark against an international best-practice standard. The over-staffing problem within the SOEs is attributed to the then prevailing state regulations which imposed obligations on enterprises in the way surplus workers were to be treated. Unlike many other countries, divesting companies or sellers are liable for severance payments in China even if the predator company or buyer offers employment to the employees of the seller, regardless of whether the terms and conditions of employment that are offered are similar or even more favourable. This begs the question as to the point in time where the obligation of having to pay severance compensation by the selling company is to be fulfilled. There are cases in third-tier cities where workers staged demonstrations at government offices to protest against the failure to pay severance compensations following an acquisition of a state-owned business by a foreign entity. Assuming that such compensations are duly paid, it then raises another question as to whether the service period that the employee has with the SOE is to be recognised and thus treated as being continuous service upon being taken on by the newly formed company. According to Clifford Chance, an international legal consulting firm in China commenting on employee issues in China M&A deals, 'foreign companies which are targeting Chinese enterprises for M&A deals should take note that a resettlement plan which provides for between 70 and 80 per cent of the employees from the target company absorbed into the newly formed joint venture or wholly owned foreign company will not normally be challenged'.

Up to this point, the discussion centres on staffing levels and the problem of over-staffing. There is an unusual situation where employees who are not part of the headcount of the target M&A company are working for the company. These are shared services employees who may be employed at corporate or group level. Employees on shared services must never be ignored as these services are necessary when the management takeover is concluded. Examples of these shared services are payroll, security, maintenance of common premises, and management and maintenance of shared facilities (such as cinema, hospital, medical clinic, canteen, state-assigned housing). A useful manner of looking at this particular issue is to categorise all these services into the following:

1. Services which are dedicated for the M&A target company application, e.g. payroll. This is likely to be an area where the foreign party may have a strong preference to manage the payroll function on its own. If such is the intent, then arrangements should be made for the transfer of the appropriate payroll administration employees to the target M&A company.

2. Services which can be shared, e.g. canteen, medical clinic, housing maintenance, etc. To achieve effective economies of scale, it may be better to leave these services on a shared basis and negotiate on the equitable costs to share.

3. Services which cannot be taken over, e.g. main entrance security, cinema, school facilities, hospital running, maintenance of common areas, etc. For these services, the issue to look at is whether these could be dispensed with (e.g. cinema facilities which could be replaced with additional benefits which the SOE does not provide) or the company could provide a monetary benefit for the

individual employees to take care of it themselves (e.g. medical facilities). Negotiations for costs sharing need to take into consideration what is and what is not provided.

Xia Gang (下岗) or Nei Tui (内退) employees

It is rather difficult to translate the Chinese ideas of *xia gang* or *nei tui* into English. The term 'gang' refers to the position that a person holds in a company, e.g. engineer, accountant, salesman, electrician, etc. In the Chinese context, a position is distinct and separate from an employment relationship. A position that one is assigned to refers only to a work relationship where one's role and responsibilities are defined. An employment relationship is a legal contract that outlines the remuneration that one is eligible to enjoy, with the attendant benefits and the terms to be complied with. Owing to this separation, it is thus possible for the work relationship to be terminated without the legal employment relationship being adversely affected, which means it continues to remain in service. Such a situation is unthinkable in Westernised corporations as the elimination of a position would simply imply the termination of the employment relationship of the employee with the company. Of course, there may be instances in a Western industrial landscape where a position holder is either temporarily suspended or on long-term paid or partially paid or unpaid leave due to medical reasons. In such cases, the position remains as an organisational headcount, notwithstanding the fact that the position holder is not on the job in the interim period. In the Chinese situation, the position is rendered redundant and thus would not be accounted for or reflected in the organisation chart. So it is virtually a contradiction in that the person is legally employed but not working at the contractual workplace. This is what 'xia gang' technically amounts to. In the event that a vacancy for a similar position should arise in the future, then the company is obliged to recall the *xia gang* employee.

Nei tui can be simply translated as 'internal retirement'. Technically speaking, the arrangement is very similar to a *xia gang* situation in that the person no longer has a position in the company but continues to enjoy an employment relationship. Moreover, the termination of service is permanent from the point of view that there is no obligation on the part of the company to re-offer the *nei tui* person full-time employment in the future should a suitable vacancy arise. The difference between a *xia gang* or *nei tui* employee and a full-time employee is in the remuneration package, besides the fact of reporting or not reporting for work on a daily work basis. *Xia gang* or *nei tui* employees are paid a reduced monthly salary (the ratio being dependent upon seniority and years of service) and reduced benefits. The primary objective of adopting this *xia gang* or *nei tui* practice is to cushion the hardship of affected employees who were so accustomed to an iron-clad rice bowl. Instead of feeling pain, this very ingenious Chinese *xia gang/nei tui* method actually makes the Chinese employees feel protected since their pension and medical insurance continue to be covered and their salaries continue to be paid, albeit at a reduced level. Since they feel they are being taken care of, the risk of a public demonstration taking place is thus negated.

In conducting an HR due diligence, effort should be directed towards confirming the following information:

1. Whether there are *xia gang* or *nei tui* employees on the payroll. If so, what is the cost impact as a percentage of total payroll?

2. In which payroll are these costs captured? (in the business unit itself or absorbed in a group level payroll, which

means that looking at the books of the target unit will not uncover any of these category of employees).

3. How many *xia gang* or *nei tui* employees are there?

4. Were these employees all made redundant at the same time or in different phases?

5. Have you carried out a retirement-by-year analysis of these employees (so as to be aware of the costs-by-year and for how many years into the future they need to be carried)?

6. Has any commitment been given to the present employees that future plans will not include any redundancy? Any such commitment will pose a major constraint to operational efficiency.

Scrutiny of job descriptions

Job descriptions (JD) provide insights into the overall objectives, roles, responsibilities, limits of authority, reporting/peer relationships, critical success factors and competencies for the respective positions within the business unit. Although job descriptions offer a view of work in the organisation, it is important to remember that they may not be an HR tool that the target M&A company relies on. The other possibility is that the JD format may not be comprehensive as the one that is commonly used by multinational corporations. Notwithstanding this minor shortcoming, HR practitioners should still look for ways to understand the roles that each position plays in the overall scheme of things. Taking a worst-case scenario, let us assume that the particular target unit has no JD documentation, and the only way to gain an understanding is by way of dialogue with three parties, namely the senior manager of each position, the position holder and the HR leader. Such dialogues are opportunities to gain an awareness of how the business is managed, the depth of knowledge of the business and the trends (both domestic and global) that affect the business as well as the competencies of each management team member. A JD, whether evidenced by way of a document or through dialogue sessions or probing questioning, provides one platform from which assessments can be made of the organisational strengths or shortcomings, potential risks, quality of management, internal control management and authority structure. A stress test of each JD against the job holder may be conducted to determine the gaps, which may include competencies, real authority being exercised, accountability as measured against responsibilities, understanding of the role and objectives, and its contribution to the business performance.

Systems integrity and continuity

In terms of human resource technology, it is important to probe the degree of computerisation that has been applied to capture HR information and to determine the ease with which the information system can be integrated. This step is especially critical once the foreign party takes over the task of management of the information from an agreed target date. Of singular importance is the payroll system as it entails compensating the takeover employees in a timely manner. In a situation where not all employees from the SOE are to be taken over by the newly formed company, whether it is a joint venture or a wholly foreign-owned enterprise, the corresponding adjustments must be made to the human resource information system so that the updated and accurate data are appropriately reflected.

There are two issues which need to be addressed in relation to the HR information system. The first is the question of system compatibility and the second is the need to port the human resource information at a given timeframe. The first question can be addressed by the company's internal information systems expertise. The second can be resolved through a mutual agreement with the Chinese party to provide continued payroll services for an interim period (say from three to six months following takeover of management). For this arrangement to comply with corporate governance, authorisation procedures must be put into place before the necessary payment is made.

Security

Security as discussed in this context refers to physical security. It may not always be the case that the target company is only a fringe unit sited within an industrial complex. Whether the target is a stand-alone unit with its own perimeter fence or security wall, or whether it is located within a large complex, an understanding of the security layout will be useful. The most basic security concern stems from where the various control points are. These are the points at which ingress into and egress from the premises are managed and controlled. Beyond control points, the next area to look into would be security layers. Security layers are aimed at preventing security breach and thus should withstand a stress test to ensure that a break-in will be an unlikely event. The way this works is that should an intruder manage to breach the initial layer, the intruder will then encounter the second and subsequent layers of security. An example is that the perimeter fence provides the first line of security and this is supplemented by strategic siting of cameras as a second line followed by manned patrolling as a third line and so forth. One must not forget the maxim that the tighter the security, the higher will be the security costs and the greater the inconvenience caused to users of the facilities. It is thus pertinent to ask whether the nature of one's industry needs such sophisticated security measures that are in place. But if the target unit is the fringe business of the group and is sited right in the centre of the complex, and where the core business of the group requires this extensive security network, the question of cost sharing may become an issue as the needs are conflicting. In this situation, the foreign entity or JV does not need an elaborate security system but the SOE or Chinese business does. This is compounded by the fact that the M&A target cannot be physically segregated for the purpose of creating its own independent ingress and egress routes for both its employees and vehicles (which include suppliers and contractors, other than its own fleet). No matter what the actual situation is and how complex the issue can be, the question of right of access must be addressed before the signing of the M&A agreement. This is even more true in the case of an acquisition.

On the other hand, one must also be aware that the Chinese party's current security system may not be adequate to meet the demands of the foreign business. In this instance, negotiations need to focus on the right to construct a perimeter fence around the premises.

The legal perspective

Scrutiny of employment contracts

Prior to reviewing employment contracts, it is important to understand, at the outset, the manner in which employees are categorised, such as full-time employees, part-time employees, casual workers, fixed-term contract employees, seconded employees, employees-on-loan, *xia gang/nei tui* employees, trainees or interns, and any other groupings that do not fall within those outlined above. Conduct an inventory of the headcount to determine if any single grouping exceeds 3 per cent of the total workforce; any category that exceeds the 3 per cent limit should be scrutinised closely and analysed further. For the management team, a complete analysis is necessary. The vetting of every individual employment contract needs to be carried out. This is for the purpose of uncovering any contract terms which are non-standard or are specifically applicable to the position holder. For non-standard terms in the contract, the purpose is to examine the implications of these terms, from the perspective both of costs and of tenure. An understanding of the background to justify such terms will certainly be useful. Stress tests on governance or ethical issues need to be performed. For the next level of staff (which is probably the senior executive level), it is recommended that a one-third sampling of the contracts be conducted. For the remaining staff, a 10 per cent sampling of the contracts will be sufficient to provide information on contractual obligations and costs implications. Non-standard terms in employment contracts are an unlikely issue in SOEs, but it is always a good habit to be in the know rather than being caught unawares. A comparative study of the differences in benefits among differing seniority levels will give an idea of the type and degree of benefit enhancements when an employee moves from one level to the next higher level.

When reviewing employment contracts, an appropriate question is 'which particular contract is the right one to scrutinise?' What this question raises is that as a person progresses along a career path, it is most likely that many of them would have been given different job assignments (whether by way of promotion to a higher level position or by transfer to a different department altogether or even a transfer/secondment to a different business unit). Technically, a new contract would have been put in place with every significant career change along the path. For a comprehensive investigation of the employment contracts, a focus on the latest two contract terms is adequate.

Scrutiny of HR policies, systems and procedures

For a start, it is important to determine if the HR policies and procedures of the organisation have been documented in a written form, or established through entrenched work practice. If the policies and procedures are embedded as work habits, it can be an insurmountable task to uncover all the entrenched work practices. Notwithstanding the difficulty, it is imperative to understand the purpose and objectives of each and every HR policy and procedure in order to determine if there are unacceptable or undesirable practices in place. If the HR policies and procedures are prescribed in a written form, it is useful to verify if these policies and procedures are also included in an employee handbook or HR manual or are issued as periodic updates. The next step of the scrutiny is to examine the approval process. This requires an understanding of the manner by which policies and procedures are formulated; the position holders who are responsible for drafting them; the position holders that review and approve the policies and procedures; the documentation process and finally, the communication process that highlights the way policies and procedures are being filtered to the shopfloor. The role of HR (in terms of deciding what areas to review or introduce, the degree of influence being exerted and the relationship with other functions) is an indicator of the style of management in the organisation.

The next area to observe is the contents of the employee handbook or policy manual. Are the human resource procedures overwhelmingly administrative-driven or do they seek to balance between administration and management processes (which provide data and information to guide employees in their performance). As an example, consider the way leaves of absence, such as sick leave or injury leave or annual leave or unpaid leave are administratively driven. However, a section on performance management which delves into the company's values, business directions, strategy and objectives to key performance indicators, critical success factors and measurement and finally indicators for future development are process-driven. If present-day HR is purely administrative, then an assessment is required to determine whether and how quickly HR will be transformed into a strategic role in the near future so that HR can partner the business in bringing strategy and business directions to fruition.

Core HR systems to examine are compensation, performance management, training & development and succession planning. Is information relating to all these systems based on formal software systems which capture decisions in a structured manner? Or is it a situation where one will be told that such systems do exist in SOEs except that they do not rely on software technology to structure all information relating to these subject matters? There is a likelihood that the foreign party may end up renovating the HR systems to align them to their global specifications or standards. The aim of examining the core HR systems is to determine the depth of HR knowledge and, where necessary, to assess the steps in filling the competency gaps.

Extraneous contractual obligations

Contractual obligations are provided in addition to the terms or conditions of the employment contract, and as the term would imply, must be complied with or fulfilled. In such a situation, the question of what constitutes 'contractual obligations' becomes important. Can such obligations be given verbally and can claims on contractual obligations be legally binding? If the obligations are explicitly documented and the commitment is unambiguous, then it is clear what is necessary and indisputable. In a situation where there is documentary evidence of these obligations and where the foreign party is felt to be dominant, what then is the recourse? Can these obligations be nullified? This should be made an item for negotiations. But claims of a verbal commitment raise a different set of challenges. It is irrelevant whether the commitment given relates to a promotion, salary adjustment, special bonus/incentive, additional benefits or extraneous payments. What is important is to ensure that there are no undue payments or cost implications that are outstanding and awaiting payment. To prevent a contentious and vexatious issue from arising, a feasible solution is to extract a written undertaking from the Chinese that there were no such commitments given on a verbal basis to any of the employees who are to be transferred to the newly formed company and that in the event of any future claim made by any of the employees, such claims will remain the liability of the Chinese party. This would thus relieve the foreign party of responsibility for any of these unknown or unseen factors.

Outstanding payments

Outstanding payments are payments which the employees are eligible to receive at a future date and at the material time of handing/taking over management, when some of these payments are yet to be paid, they would become outstanding claims. This question of liability, although obvious, should be unambiguously agreed to avoid any disputes with employees from arising or creating problems for employees after they are transferred to the newly formed company. These payments can take many forms and may arise from differing conditions. Payments could be work performance-related (e.g. overtime, sales commission), profit-related (e.g. bonus) and/or claims-related (e.g. reimbursements arising from pursuit of business such as transport, meals for extended hours worked). It is unlikely that payments due will be settled before the handing over date. Hence, it is important that, at the negotiations phase, an understanding be reached whereby a mechanism is put into place for final settlement of all outstanding payments in order to minimise disruption to work continuity.

Internal controls

Authorisation policy

A company's authorisation policy is an indicator of good governance and its effectiveness in internal control. In studying the policy, it is important to determine the structure of the internal control policy. The segregation between expenditure and claims should be examined. As an example, it is insightful to examine how capital expenditure and consumables expenditure are allocated. When studying the claims process and procedures, it is necessary to verify whether all the various approved claims made are supported by official documentary evidence, and made in accordance with the policy guidelines. In other words, the employee making the claims must do so within an acceptable timeframe (and not with tax invoices for expenditure which were incurred in the previous financial year, for instance) and the supervisory manager must have approved the claims on the basis that these had been appropriately incurred or pre-approved and further ensuring that the quantum of claims are within constraints imposed by prevailing policies. In a case in Wuhan, a sales manager on-site made two claims for entertainment expenses. Both the tax invoices were issued by the same restaurant and were dated three weeks apart. In addition, the two invoices were consecutively numbered. Technically, it would have implied that the restaurant had no business transaction for the entire three weeks from the first occasion he entertained his guests at this restaurant to the very next time that he did so. One other fact that was cited was that the total expenditure that was incurred was comparatively higher than a similar standard restaurant in Shanghai, which did not make good sense as the cost of living in Shanghai then was significantly higher. When questioned, the sales manager explained that he was drunk on the first occasion and did not ask for a tax invoice then and only got one when he returned there for the second entertainment. As for the excessively high price, the explanation given was that female companions were engaged even though this was not approved prior to the entertainment. This case is quoted as a lesson to be learned of the kind of claims that could be made and approved, no matter how dubious these might be. It also revealed the kinds of laxity in audits in the approval process. On this particular occasion, the supervising manager was a Westernised expatriate who did not understand or read Hanyu, and that exacerbated matters such as reimbursement claims. On the flip side of claims made would be the approval process. Efforts should be made to determine if the limits imposed on the various levels of authority satisfy effective internal control requirements. One principle to rely on is that of reasonableness, whereby a balance is maintained between expediency and operational efficiency as measured against tightness in control. An overly tight process will create an administrative burden whereas an expedient procedure will create opportunities for abuse. A well-managed system will thus feature functional responsibilities (that is, clearly demarcated departments being responsible for given work processes), levels of responsibility (that is, stipulating the seniority level at which staff are authorised to approve certain work processes) and limits of authority (that is, at each specific level, the specified limits by which a position holder is permitted to sign off a given work process).

HR-related claims

HR-related claims would commonly include overtime, transport, medical expenses, meals, entertainment, business trips (both local and overseas), and all forms of allowances. It is good practice to pay special attention to the authorisation process (that is, to establish whether claims are properly verified against actual occurrence) and in appropriate instances to carry out a stress test, e.g. overtime payments against production volumes. This will provide an indication of either the effective control or laxity of management.

Company seal or chop

In China, the company seal or chop, as it is more commonly known, represents the legal endorsement or approval of any official document. Legally, the entire assets of a business unit can be signed off or transferred out in the extreme case of a chop being abused or misused, whether wilfully or otherwise. The first point of control to ensure appropriate usage would be to decide the custodian for the chop. Needless to say, the person appointed as the chop custodian must be trustworthy, of a certain seniority level and predominantly desk-bound. Business dynamics are invariably subject to the vagaries of change and twists and turns. One common problem, for whatever reasons, is a leave of absence of the chop custodian. The leave of absence leads to a need for a stand-in custodian. Records need to be meticulously kept to ensure that an audit trail will determine who the specific chop custodian had been who handled a given case of authorised use of the chop, if such a need should arise. A straightforward verification can be made on those days when the official chop custodian had been physically away from work and how these matters were being handled at the material point in time. Had the handover been appropriately recorded in accordance with proper procedures and had records been properly kept during this leave of absence? Where records were kept, it is insightful to examine the detailed activities captured in those records. Do the records show adequate information which enables the company to trace the origin of each given problem, i.e. the person responsible for the usage, the purpose of the usage, a brief description of the documents that were chopped, retention of the set of documents which were chopped in the archives of the custodian, the name and signature of the person authorising the use of the chop and the documentation capturing all this information. An effective way of verifying the events is to take a sample of the documents which were archived by the custodian and check these against the records to determine if proper and accurate records had been kept and if these had been appropriately approved. Since the official chop is of such vital importance to the conduct of business in China, it thus also leads to the issue of what is the ideal level of authority to authorise the use of this mechanism. This company chop issue is further complicated and aggravated by a complex organisational structure which straddles the entire country where small stand-alone entities exist in lower tier cities. As the business contribution and impact these entities bring are seen to be inconsequential, these are potential areas that are not monitored regularly and closely. In addition, the person managing the business unit is relatively junior even though his designation appears to be more senior as he is managing the entire business for that location. Therefore, it is imperative for policy decision makers to consider this point when deciding an authorisation model to rely on.

Where the nature of the business of the target company requires a significant proportion of dealings to be conducted outside the premises, e.g. trading, project management and off-site operations, the question relates to whether the chop could be taken outside the company premises to seal documents at the official conclusion of a business deal. This is obviously a delicate business situation where the possible abuse of the chop is both real and likely. This is a good indicator of control in usage of the chop. Our experience in dealing with this aspect of control is to prohibit such a practice. Moreover, such a practice of prohibition is common among companies in China. It is better to be inconvenient and allow some delay in concluding a business deal than to face the unknown prospects and consequences of an abuse in using the company chop. Expediency should not be an adequate justification for lack of control in this instance.

To illustrate the importance of the company chop, we would like to highlight another case involving the abuse of the chop which happened in a third tier city. In this case, the official chop was handed to a supplier as a guarantee for overdue payments. What happened was that the company proceeded to make a replacement chop. This is an extremely risky and unacceptable manner of coping with a business situation. As things stood, this was not 'seen' during the due diligence phase and was discovered after the deal had been signed and management handover effected. Although the case may appear to be uncommon, it nevertheless goes to show that the most unexpected thing can go seriously wrong. It is a good habit not to have an ingrained mindset that things are what they appear on the surface. HR due diligence teams should probe deeply to ascertain if there had been any known cases of abuse of the company chop. It is also insightful to examine the actions that had been taken in those known cases and assess whether those actions correspond with the severity of each case. This will help determine the code of conduct and behavioural standards imposed by the company.

Leave administration

The comprehensiveness of leave records will provide an indication on how HR manages the various kinds of leave of absence. Leave can be categorised into annual, medical, hospitalisation, compassionate, maternity, staff injury, festival, authorised unpaid and unauthorised unpaid. Being careless in administering all forms of leave of absence can only lead to a laxity in behavioural standards, bad habits and, worst of all, abuses. All unacceptable and/or undesirable work habits pose barriers to change when new standards of behaviour and corporate values are put in place. When behaviour becomes deeply entrenched, it will become an acceptable standard and this will reinforce the resistance to change that one desires to bring about. Thus it is vital that this be factored into any change programme that one plans to initiate upon management takeover.

Work attendance

The management of workforce attendance depends on the nature of the industry. When inspecting work attendance records, the area to focus on will be what is commonly termed as direct and indirect staff, normally defined as those groups of employees which impact the core business and whose tasks are performed as an integral team. For example, in manufacturing industry, the production or operations staff will be categorised as direct employees, and in trading, the sales or logistics staff will be clustered as direct staff. This grouping of trading as direct staff does not suggest that the general and administration staff do not have an impact on business, but rather that their work need not be collectively and simultaneously performed all the time. Work attendance controls (e.g. clocking cards or security access cards) serve as effective tools to manage employees' presence at the workplace. On the other hand, the lack of an effective control system indicates management laxity and is an area for concern.

Disciplinary procedures and cases

The legal systems and judiciary of a country mirror the work ethics and code of conduct of organisations. Without a transparent and fair system that is universally applied to all strata of society, its citizens may feel insecure. Similarly, for a corporation without clearly defined ethics and guidelines for acceptable behavioural standards, undesirable work habits and misconduct will be the norm. In addition to the values and behavioural codes of a company, another aspect of ethics and code of conduct is the way misconduct is dealt with. This includes the process of dealing with misconduct, the manner in which misconduct cases are adjudicated, and the manner by which judgments and decisions are taken and recorded. It is necessary to identify dissatisfaction arising from favouritism, nepotism and discriminatory treatment, which only serves to engender ill-feeling and low morale among other employees. Upon the takeover of management, such issues should not be allowed to continue as misconduct can develop into deep-seated grievances. It is best that these kinds of issues be expediently dealt with in the first instance.

In conducting HR due diligence, it is necessary to examine past cases of disciplinary infringements and determine how these had been historically handled and dispensed with. It is not necessary to investigate all cases; just a sampling of a selection of incidences will suffice. The purpose is to get an adequate grasp of the situation and the way cases are managed.

Performance management

As a management tool, performance management shares a common platform with talent management and rewards system in a company. The entire management process yields large amounts of information on the philosophy, values, management style, work ethics, business strategy, delivery of results and its importance attached to employees. At the core of performance management is the process of setting goals. How are these strategic goals determined, how are they filtered downwards (e.g. from a corporate level to the business group level and finally to the business unit level) and how are these eventually translated into department key deliverables? What are the information measurements used to indicate whether desired results have been achieved? What is the degree of intervention given to managers to apply when performance is not heading in the desired direction? How are individual employees' personal goals reconciled with organisational objectives? Are there transparent or hidden forces embedded in the performance management process? The answers to all these questions will provide an insight into how performance management is applied to facilitate the effective delivery of strategic and operational goals.

By contrast, discrepancy arises when achieved results are below the expectation of the desired outcomes. This may imply that the performance of the individual employee or team or department has fallen into the category where performance improvement is necessary. An understanding of the process used to address performance improvement is therefore necessary. How performance gaps are identified; how this vital information is communicated to the person or team, and how the improvement plan is formulated, implemented and monitored are matters that should be dealt with.

The costs perspective

Employment and payroll control

In managing costs, the first thing to inspect is the manner by which the monthly payroll is computed and duly authorised before payment is made. For the fixed portion of the payroll record, i.e. the basic salary, it is important to compare the total basic pay for the selected months against the corresponding headcount report. Are monthly variances substantiated by staff movements, i.e. staff attrition or staff increase? For the variable component of the payroll, an analysis into the computation of overtime payments is necessary. On overtime payments, it is important to examine the authorisation and control process. A reliable test is to conduct a six to twelve month overtime payment analysis against production volumes over the same period to reveal the consistency. Do overtime payments closely correspond with fluctuations in output? Another aspect of the overtime analysis is to look at overtime payment as a percentage of total payrolls. If the percentage is consistently in excess of 20 per cent of total basic salary payroll, then it is only appropriate to probe further to determine whether there is an under-staffing issue (an unlikely scenario in most cases of SOEs) or whether it is a case of lax control.

The next step is to study the components that constitute the gross salary and conduct a payroll analysis. The breakdown of all salary items, such as salary related, non-salary (i.e. other monetary components which are not related to salary, e.g. incentive and allowances) and statutory costs (e.g. pension fund contribution, unemployment funds, medical insurance, provident fund, etc.) should be examined. The purpose is to determine whether the various statutory contributions are computed in accordance with statutory regulations that govern each of the pay items. There are useful ratios which can be applied to see how employment costs stack up against sales revenue, gross profit (rather than net profits as taxation rates can affect such ratios) and compare these against similar ratios which are derived from other countries with similar or comparable production or commercial capacity.

Benefits administration

When studying the company benefits, the first hurdle is to verify if the eligibility criteria are strictly guided by a policy manual or embedded in all employment contracts. Where benefits are regulated by statutory provisions such as statutory contributions, it is necessary to ensure that there are no legal compliance issues as major infringements of the law of the land can lead to significant liabilities being imposed by the authorities. From years of experience and exposure to conducting HR due diligence, it is evident, as an example, that a privately owned company in Beijing was involved in under-declaration of salaries with the intention of making lower statutory contributions and reducing costs.

A results-driven approach which can be used to achieve time optimisation is to target high-cost benefit items. Three core benefits that fall within the high-costs benefit category are the provision of a company car, business entertainment claims and family benefits. The key concern is the constraints that are imposed on an employee enjoying or consuming such benefits. The procedural and distribution justice in implementation and the consistency by which policy constraints are adhered to are symptoms of perceived fairness in management practices. Where there is widespread perceived inequality, it can only deteriorate into employee grievances when there is a change in management.

Compensation management

A major portion of employee salaries or staff costs form part of the fixed component of overall employment costs. Salary adjustments dictate the increased costs and financial burden that companies incur annually. An effective way to understand the way compensation is managed is to inspect the salary adjustments/increases procedures that are put in place. The entire approval process, beginning with the salary and related costs budgeting, fact-finding, recommendation for salary increase for the year in question to final approval, will reveal how salaries are managed and controlled, the level of importance attached to employees' career growth and the way employees' contributions are recognised and rewarded. How are rewards linked to contribution and how are assessments weighted? Do performance records correspond closely to actual rewards (which can take the form of incentive bonuses or promotion or salary increases) given?

All these questions will give an indication of the compensation philosophy adopted by the target company.

Training costs

Training is an integral part of the learning and development and succession planning process. Talent development, skills enhancement and bridging of competency gaps of employees are human resource interventions in global corporations. What differs among the global corporations and the local companies are the focus on management as compared with functional training and the training costs as a ratio of total employment costs. While conducting a diligence audit on a training plan and its related costs, the areas to explore are the contents of the training plan, how training needs are identified and approved, the emphasis on management as compared to functional training and most importantly, the focus given to development training as compared to training to address immediate gaps or business needs. The analysis of the training plan and its implementation will reveal the training philosophy that the company adopts.

Administration processes and procedures

Whether the administration function is within the HR jurisdiction is not relevant to the discussion. What is more important to examine as part of an HR due diligence exercise are high cost items such as vehicle fleet management. The efficiency with which the company manages its vehicle fleet can easily be determined by the control it imposes. As an example, the controls are as follows:

- petrol consumption
- tyre change

- maintenance and repair
- vehicle usage and authorisation process
- comparative performance among vehicles within the fleet.

In managing the high costs of administration, it may be useful to conduct an analysis of the 'buy versus lease' option in order to determine which option is viable for respective businesses.

Shared services and facilities

In the context of a SOE conglomerate, shared services would typically include security of the infrastructure, transport, uniforms, dining halls, schools, entertainment outlets (such as cinemas), medical clinics, building maintenance, housing maintenance (separate from buildings as housing refers to apartment units which were previously allocated by the state) and road maintenance. It is likely that costs relating to all these items are captured in the group's accounts and not charged to the operating units. This would certainly constitute an unseen cost. It cannot be assumed that these costs will continue to be absorbed after M&A. In fact, the reverse will be the likely situation. Costs sharing of shared services is best resolved and agreed upon before the M&A deal is signed and sealed. Another probable outcome is that the foreign party may not want to continue providing some of these benefits, such as cinema tickets or schooling for employees' children as most foreign companies would consider these as items of personal responsibility rather than corporate responsibility. If this is the case, then the best thing to do is to list all these shared facilities and agree on those which should continue and those to be discontinued.

5

Navigating beyond relationships

Abstract: The concept of 'hidden' or in many cases, 'unseen' is usually construed with untruthful intentions and/or bad behaviours. In contrast, the notion of 'unseen', as espoused by the Chinese people signifies truthful behaviours or acts that are tacit, unobserved or unnoticeable until it is uncovered with experience and relevant expertise. It is necessary to extend beyond affective relationships to understand what is truthfully unseen in assessing risks. Risk assessment includes identification; description; assessment; and the formulation of the mitigation plan.

Key words: unseen, risks assessment, 'one-person, two-employment relationships', behavioural related risks, likelihood, impact, mitigation plan, manageability, timeliness

Being truthful

As we reflect on the objectives for conducting HR due diligence in China, there are two key concepts that are pertinent and specific to the Chinese. These apply to the notions of 'unseen' as in people cost and the cultural nuances. In navigating beyond relationships, it is necessary to unpack the meaning of 'unseen', particularly in the state-owned sector, by drawing attention to the idea of 'unseen' as interpreted by the non-Chinese. Contrary to popular beliefs, unseen may not necessarily connote 'hidden' as in agendas. In a negative sense, the concept of 'hidden' would imply a deliberate act of concealment. For the Chinese 'unseen' could mean acts or practices that are either implicit, tacit, not known explicitly, unobserved, or not made noticeable until they are uncovered by experience and relevant expertise.

This point is aptly described by Simon Winchester in his recent book, *The Man Who Loved China*. Winchester wrote about Needham, a Cambridge biochemistry don, who was so captivated by China that he went on an intellectual pursuit across war-torn and far-flung Chinese outposts to gather evidence on scientific and technological innovations invented by the Chinese. The first half of the twentieth century in China, according to Winchester, was widely perceived by foreigners with disdain, contempt and utter exasperation. However, Needham's perception of China was to change drastically after he witnessed an elaborate tree grafting technique that was carried out very differently from the techniques he was familiar with. As a scientist, Needham has acute observation skills, honed by his scientific training on the necessity for empirical evidence. What started off as an observation for Needham led him to realise that tree grafting as performed in China derived from thousands of years of practice, pre-dating the technique that is taken for granted in his native country. Based on Needham's pursuits, among others, Winchester concludes that the Chinese did things very differently in China. Needham did not hastily conclude that the Chinese have an inferior or non-standard way of doing things; they merely do them very differently, perhaps leveraging on Chinese cultural nuances. The lesson drawn from Winchester's comment is that to label the Chinese as being untruthful and inferior is unkind.

Needham's experience may be applicable within an industry or a commercial context in China. Frequently, it is not as things would appear to the non-Chinese, in that the Chinese did not intend to mislead or hide, but rather have done things differently. As an example, certain shared costs are not commonly captured in the accounting books of a business unit but charged at the sub-group or sector level. So if one relies on a familiar and perhaps Westernised accounting method of apportioning costs, it is possible that critical financial information may be overlooked. This way of looking at things from a perspective that one is trained in, over years in a Westernised work environment, probably constitutes the greatest hazard when conducting risk assessments in China.

HR risk assessment

As discussed in Chapter 3, the HR-related risks are grouped into three areas, namely costs, management, and behaviour. The unseen costs in these areas are as follows.

Cost-related risks

Shared costs

Shared costs may include items such as payroll, transport, housing maintenance, schooling facilities, medical facilities, uniforms, infrastructure and entertainment facilities, and security and canteen facilities. As an operational concept, shared costs are usually contained in large industries with numerous business or production units so that economies of scale can be optimally achieved through the pooling of common functions or needs. As an accounting concept, the

Chinese have a different way of dealing with shared costs. The fact that the costs are there cannot be altered and these need to be captured in its accounting books. A probable risk is in an inability to locate where shared costs are captured. More importantly, it is necessary to determine if the shared costs are charged out to respective users of the shared facilities. The impact of the risks on shared costs may be significant if it continues to be unseen.

Payroll

For example, in unseen payroll costs, it is abundantly clear that work stoppages or disruptions occur if payroll is not computed, and wages are not paid because its shared payroll costs are not appropriately proportioned. Even if workers return to work within a short time after the matter is resolved, the impact arising from work stoppages, and/or disruptions, besides causing a production loss, will result in an erosion of confidence in a foreign-managed enterprise. In a worst case situation, omissions in payroll computation and wage payment happen at the setting up of the JV if unseen payroll is left undiscovered.

Salary adjustments and promotions

As soon as information on an impending M&A deal gets out to the shop-floor of a business unit, it is common to find workers expecting a much higher level of compensation and benefits. In a worst case scenario, management get entangled in a consequent expectation of a better salary package as well. Ultimately, a company-wide general salary increase adjustment and promotions and/or commitment to an increase in salary after the M&A deal is concluded become necessary to appease employees. Regardless, expectations of better compensation and benefits for all employees drive an increase in costs even before the newly formed unit goes into business.

Outstanding claims by employees

Outstanding claims may take many forms: unpaid overtime, unpaid allowances, shortfall in salary payments, or reimbursements yet to be paid. The most troublesome kind of employee claims would be those relating to promised payments that are yet to be fulfilled. It does not matter what forms the outstanding claims may take. While it is important to verify the authenticity of claims by employees, a possible approach is to agree on a fundamental principle that whatever liabilities arise before the effective takeover date should be the sole responsibility of the target company. It is wise not to leave matters unspecified or which give rise to conflicting claims being asserted by any one party. The Chinese labour arbitration process normally relies heavily on documentary evidence. What is left unseen may be difficult to present in a court of law.

Company transport

In the case of company-provided transport to move employees from home to workplace and vice versa, the same due diligence should apply. Although it may be a common practice for long-established and huge Chinese state-owned conglomerates (one needs to be mindful that before the 1990s, virtually all enterprises in China were state-owned) to build housing apartments for employees in close proximity to industrial complexes, which precludes the necessity for a transport provision, it is nevertheless, a useful standard to include company transport in the risks assessment checklist. All these apartments would obviously need regular maintenance to keep them in habitable condition. Before any merger or acquisition, all such work would fall within the ambit of the group. When an operating unit is hived off or merged with a foreign enterprise, the Chinese realise that they cannot continue to be responsible for these obligations.

State-assigned housing

State-assigned housing may create challenges for M&A. This pertains to the issue of a residual value of each apartment unit that had been assigned to employees. From the experience of the authors, residual values of apartment units are not entered in the books of the business units on which the authors had undertaken HR due diligence. This is probably due to the fact that the apartments, once assigned, were no longer considered as state or enterprise assets. Neither were there any written contractual obligations on these accommodations between parties. Nevertheless, the fact that there was nothing written does not quite mean that this is not an issue. Even if the foreign party is willing to compensate for these housing units, there is the issue of determining an equitable residual value as valuations of the units differ in floor areas and were assigned in different years.

Facilities

Besides providing homes for their employees, it is also common to find Chinese industrial conglomerates building entertainment complexes such as cinemas, or educational facilities such as schools, or medical facilities such as hospitals, or welfare facilities such as canteens/cafeterias, to cater to the needs of their tens of thousands of employees. In most instances, these are shared facilities. Following a merger or acquisition of a business unit, the issue of sharing facilities to continue without a corresponding sharing of the costs of running them remains pertinent. Even if this issue is not raised by the Chinese party during the entire M&A process, it may not remain as a dormant issue in perpetuity.

Employee accessibility

Then there are also roads which traverse the vast compound of all these industrial complexes and these form ingress and egress routes, with multi-point security control/ checkpoints, leading into the particular business unit which is your M&A target. The right of way of these routes (for employees, suppliers and other stakeholders) is but one of a few potential issues. All such amenities need constant maintenance or even upgrading over time. The moment some of its businesses effectively get hived off, partially or fully, the question will arise as to whether the Chinese will continue to allow the JV or foreign enterprise employees to enjoy such benefits. Failure to resolve all these can bring about adverse impact on the employees once the management takeover is carried out and on top of that, remain a bone of contention in the future.

Management-related risks

Excessive headcount

Moving away from a macro-level, intra-group, inter-business unit focus to a micro-level, intra-business unit focus, we shall now shift to the management-related risks. The most important management issue is headcount. It is generally assumed and widely accepted that the headcount in a state-owned enterprise is very much higher than that in a business unit in the Westernised managed organisation. Many Westernised trained business managers hold the opinion that the overall payroll costs, that is, wages, allowances plus statutory contributions, of Chinese workers are relatively low as compared to those in Westernised organisations. Hence, they adopt a view from a costs standpoint by taking a rather dismissive and a highly tolerant attitude towards this issue of excessive manning levels. From a human resource perspective, the critical aspect is to adopt a productivity lens. In productivity versus costs, the more difficult element to manage is productivity as it is directly connected to ingrained habits. Work habits, especially those which are etched over many years, can be difficult to unlearn. The other risk stems from the mindset that regards job security as an unbreakable iron rice bowl. The risks increase as one moves away from a first-tier city towards a more remote region or an inner province location, where alternative job opportunities are substantially reduced, or non-existent. It must be borne in mind that all parties to a merger must make alternative arrangements for the employment of the original employees of the target company. However, there is no legal provision that stipulates that all employees must be transferred to the newly merged company. This matter of worker settlement and industrial relation arrangements will be closely scrutinised by government agencies that regulate M&A deals in China. In some cases, formal consultation with the target company's workers may be necessary. While the issue of worker settlement is typically the responsibility of the target company, it is pertinent to note that the way this issue is handled may impact on the progress of the negotiations process. Closely intertwined with headcount is the legal relationship between workers and company. Two questionable practices arise herein: one is that unrelated department functions have been added to the organisation structure of this particular business unit and the other is that additional people had been 'transferred in' shortly before M&A discussions had taken place. Diligent checks will help to uncover such practice.

Social stability

The central government recognised the challenges pertaining to excessive manning levels, particularly in the state-owned sector. During Zhu Rongji's tenure of the premiership in March 1998 to March 2003, the bulging state bureaucracy and inefficient state firms were modernised, restructured and downsized. During this period, millions faced the dim prospect of losing their jobs in the state-owned enterprises or the civil service. To address potential job losses that may result in social unrest, Premier Zhu demanded the provision of financial safety nets for the unemployed. The central government recognised that it was critical that massive urban unemployment be avoided at all costs as this could lead to a huge public outcry and anti-government demonstrations, which eventually might lead to social instability. In fact, there have been cases of anti-government demonstrations which captured the attention of the Western media. This is something about which the Chinese government is sensitive. Over the years, people realised that demonstrations can be used as a weapon of bargaining, especially with the state-owned sector. As the workers in this sector have learned, anti-government demonstrations are particularly effective when staged at specific locations (e.g. close to the seat of government, be it at township or district or municipality or provincial level) and on prominent dates (e.g. National Day or during an international conference attended by foreign government officials).

Translation risks

Loss in translation highlights the lack of understanding of the cultural nuances when Chinese terms are translated syntactically rather than semantically. For those who are not proficient in the Chinese language, there is a need to exercise caution when relying on a straightforward translation of documents. This point is best illustrated with two real-life instances of a direct and straightforward translation which went seriously wrong. In the first instance, the position of plant manager (more widely known as factory or operations manager today) was translated into the Chinese language as a 'plant' as used in the flora and fauna context. This incidence occurred in the draft JV agreement drawn up by a legal office in Shanghai. In this particular instance, the incorrect translation had no material impact on the agreement but it nevertheless indicates that some Chinese have a tendency to do a word-for-word translation. In the second instance, the translation was from Chinese to English. Here again, it involves translating another position title, that of 人事经理 or HR manager. The name card that was given to one of the authors read 'Man and Thing Manager', literally translated word for word. A Westerner may read the title on the name-card with a baffled look and with no idea as to what the role entails. For someone who is able to read the Chinese characters, it is rather amusing. How did such a translation come about in the first place? Simply put, the translation was done word for word, that is, 人 means person and 事 means matter or thing and 经理 means manager. We suppose the point has been adequately driven home.

Nei tui employees

Inherent in this translation issue lies a different nature of risk and this has to do with the need to trim the unwieldy public sector staffing. As explained in the earlier section on 'Social stability', there is an urgent need to prevent any form of massive urban unemployment to maintain stability. The solution was found in an entirely unique concept with no equivalent in the Western industrialised countries. It is better known as a 'technical layoff with Chinese characteristics'. In Hanyu or the Han Chinese language, the idea is called 内退 (pronounced *neitui*) or literally translated as 'internal retirement', which can be said to be meaningless in English. Interestingly, many local Chinese HR practitioners have translated this term 'nei tui' as 'early retirement', although it conflicts with another term 早退, which has the same meaning.

From a Westernised perspective and a working definition, nei tui may be defined as a 'technical layoff'. In a Westernised environment, a permanent layoff would be tantamount to a retrenchment. In Asian countries, this legal severance of an employment relationship may result in a one-off monetary compensation in recognition of past service of retrenched employees. In the Chinese context, where the workers are transitioning from a planned economy to a market economy, a different kind of workers' protection is needed to address the issue of a loss of a job, with its attendant loss of an ongoing income stream and the continuation of medical benefits and pension fund payments. The Chinese solution lies in providing workers with the source of family assurance and comfort that continues until their official retirement age. The concept reinforces the system of lifelong care that the Communist Party had been providing since the downfall of dynastic China. This solution is akin to Deng Xiaoping's famously termed 'one country, two systems' political concept in regard to the way Hong Kong is administered.

Perhaps the concept *nei tui* can be termed 'one employee, two employment relationships'. In a *nei tui* situation, the employee continues to have that legal relationship with the company in the sense that s/he remains on the payroll. However, s/he has a different work relationship in that s/he is not contractually obliged to be present at the workplace. What the 'nei tui' concept provided was a guaranteed income at a reduced rate until the official retirement age plus medical and pension benefits in perpetuity. The *nei tui* employee has an unbreakable iron rice bowl that is looked after by the state. Although the reduction in income is painful, the element of care provided by the state remains.

The problem for a foreign enterprise is to uncover if there is a group of *nei tui* people present in their headcount data as this will potentially be a high fixed payroll cost. The common practice for state-owned enterprises is to include *nei tui* employees in the headcount statistics but have the payroll kept separate from the payroll of regular employees. It is from this standpoint that this portion of the payroll costs may be unseen when due diligence focuses mainly on regular payroll figures.

Transfer of employees upon conclusion of M&A deal

At the conclusion of the M&A deal, employees whose transfer to the newly formed company has been agreed must be transferred to the target company. Although this transfer is the sole responsibility of the target company, it is good practice to read the transfer document to ensure that no unforeseen implications of any provisions may arise in the future. The risk lies in the wording of the transfer document which may have potential future implications as well. A second reason is to ensure that there are no unnecessary or unfair commitments made which may carry future obligations. The risk impact is very dependent on the nature, scope and depth of applicability and length of the validity period.

Nature of industry

The crucial factor on the nature of the industry is the kind of impact that this causes on its neighbourhood. This would largely apply to industries like chemicals, especially those which give off a foul odour or generate an audible noise level or discharge toxic waste into the drainage system and rivers or cause a high level of truck movement. All these matters either create inconvenience for the community or cause perceived environmental damage. With an increasing awareness of the need to protect the environment, taking a sensitive attitude towards this issue is helpful. The fact that the particular plant has been there for decades does not necessarily mean that the plant will continue to operate in a problem-free environment once the business falls into the management of foreign enterprises. Raising this as an issue to be looked at and resolved will go a long way to minimising potential issues.

Role of the party secretary

In the SOEs, the party secretary assumes a senior position in the organisation and plays an active role in the management and administration of the operating unit. In terms of hierarchy, a party secretary may be senior to the general manager of the company, ostensibly owing to this party ties and party responsibilities. This issue of the role of party secretary and its attendant responsibilities need to be addressed unequivocally so that management conflicts do not arise. Nothing can be worse than a situation of an open disagreement between an expatriate general manager (who supposedly runs the business) and the local Chinese party secretary where a proposed change in business direction or strategy cannot proceed owing to such an impasse. This can only lead to ineffective and chaotic management.

Role of the trade union

In China, the formation of a union and a party apparatus are givens. Traditionally, the trade union in China has played a non-bargaining role in industries. Unions can be described as social organisations looking after the welfare of their members through organising activities such as trips, visits, arranging for funeral wakes, helping families to cope with setbacks, removal of personal belongings arising from relocation of home, etc. The role of collective bargaining is somewhat foreign to them. Over the years, the International Labour Organization has been assertive in influencing trade unions in China to introduce collective bargaining. In fact, the practice of collective bargaining in industries has already taken root in China, with companies introducing collective agreements. It will be interesting to see the collective bargaining model that China ultimately decides to rely on.

Behaviour-related risks

Unhealthy employee relations

With the focus on people-related issues, another aspect of risks is employee behaviour. For a start, it is useful to examine the strength of employee relations and to determine if there has been a history of industrial relations cases brought to arbitration. What has been the level of management awareness of this situation? What has been done to address these concerns? How effective has it been in dealing with these concerns as perceived by employees? The responses will provide an insight into the management style and culture of the target company. Management style is frequently influenced by the entrenched culture and work practices. What is important is to seek out, retain and build upon those values which are considered in alignment and stem from those which are considered as undesirable or off-tangent with one's corporate values.

Consequent employee expectations

The focus on people and behaviour will be incomplete without delving into the question of expectations. It is invariable that any whisper along the corridor of an M&A involving a foreign enterprise will raise the expectations of employees on the ground, justifiably or otherwise. Expectations normally come in the form of better remuneration, benefits, systems and procedures, progressive management, equality of treatment and recognition of performance rather than connection and more since management will be changed from a 'rule by individual' system to an egalitarian 'rule by open fairness' system. To appease some of these emotions or perceptions, there is a possibility that unwritten promises or commitments could be covertly given before an M&A exercise is completed. We find it prudent to establish that such practices have not been resorted to.

Entrenched loyalty

A somewhat related risk issue is that of entrenched loyalty. Bearing in mind that many employees of state firms have long years of service, an ensuing sense of belonging and loyalty must be expected. The corollary issue is one of conflict of interest. The first point is information flow. The flow of information per se may not constitute such a major issue. A deeper problem is with misinformation, as it gets more serious when there is a hidden agenda. A second instance arises if the products or services offered by the target company are needed by the Chinese party, either corporate or individual. It is necessary to exercise discretion and be sensitive to the point that this aversion to risk does not develop into an open display of suspicion.

Blatant flouting of state regulations

At the negative end of the behavioural spectrum is the possibility of a blatant flouting of state regulations with the purpose of reducing operational costs. As an example, a deliberate reporting of understated remuneration creates savings in an employer's statutory contributions. When one takes over the management of a business, understated remuneration for the purpose of a reduced statutory contribution leads to complex issues with government authorities; it is something that multinational corporations may want to avoid. This situation may be avoided if uncovered through due diligence checks. In addition, comparing payroll costs as shown in the financial records with similar sets of figures that appear in the HR department records may highlight the issue of understated payroll. Another method is to carry out a ratio test. This is achieved by looking at the statutory contributions under individual headings, for example, pension, unemployment, provident fund and medical insurance contributions as a percentage of the payroll. If the resultant ratios are significantly lower than overall payroll, alarm bells must ring. Having raised this risk factor, it must be said that such practices are most unlikely to be seen in state firms and are more likely to be observed in private entities.

Misuse of company chop or seal

Another practice that must be brought into focus is the way the company chop or seal is managed. In China, the company chop is required for the approval for banks to release company funds. This is where its controlled usage is of paramount importance. There are two cases in which the authors feel there are lessons to be learned on the misuse of the company chop. In the first instance, a supplier of the Chinese partner (who had no business relationship with the JV which was formed with this particular Chinese partner) needed a guarantor for separate business dealing. The Chinese partner then got the JV to act as the guarantor. What was interesting in this case was that the foreign party was not aware that such a guarantee was granted by the JV and the identity of the authority that approved this guarantee could not be traced. As things turned out, some years later, the particular supplier to the Chinese partner went bankrupt and the guarantor was jointly and severally sued by their creditors. A multi-million dollar RMB judgment was awarded by the court in favour of the creditor who took the action. At the material point in time, it could not be conclusively established as to whether it was the JV general manager or the finance manager who had authorised the release of the chop so that the guarantee could be effected. In the second case, it was more than a year after acquisition of a business unit when it was discovered that the original chop had been surrendered to a supplier to be kept as collateral against an unpaid debt. In this instance, the most serious implication is the unknown actions of the supplier to whom the chop had been surrendered. Suffice it to say, the very thought of the possible consequences is enough to send a chill all the way down the spine.

Staff retention

Staff retention is a dilemma. On the one hand, the JV acquires managerial talents in SOEs who have worked virtually all their lives in that SOE. These are the people who have in-depth technical knowledge, understand the engineering process intimately, have a good grasp of all the internal systems and organisational routines, and deal with most suppliers and customers of that generation. Unfortunately, many of these talented staff are unable to communicate in English – a vital skill highly sought by multinational corporations. Hence, the SOE's skilled staff face difficulty in communicating and working with their regional and corporate counterparts. In addition, these skilled staff have acquired a deep sense of security by working within their comfort level. Hence, it is not a question of unwillingness to move to another organisation but a situation in which there is absolutely no need to seek such a move. The catalyst to move on, that is the push factor, is simply not there. Under such circumstances, retention of talent is virtually non-existent. As the English language becomes visible in business and communication, the SOE's skilled staff begin to realise the importance of learning the language. In the coming years and among younger managers with limited exposure to the SOE style of management, the situation on retention of skilled staff will change dramatically. In a 2006 study on 'M&A in China' conducted by the Economist Intelligence Unit (EIU) in conjunction with Mercer, the three HR issues are retaining, focusing and attracting talent. Gary Wang, Mercer's M&A leader for China, commented, 'retaining key talent post-deal is absolutely essential to your China deal'.

The risk of all risks

Having discussed HR-related risks in the preceding sections, we have seen that the singular risk that will pose the biggest hurdle in achieving success of an M&A deal is assembling a competent task force or team to conduct a detailed due diligence from the legal and financial operations (including safety) and HR perspectives. The need for the presence of

HR in such a team is amplified by an observation made by Mercer in its 2009 report, 'The Human Capital Factor – M&A in China, A Focus on Value'. The 2009 report states that, 'clearly, paying a fair price is important, but focussing on another value driver – people – is of equal or greater importance as focussing on the financial demand'. The need for a specialist M&A due diligence team is eloquently articulated by Rovit et al.: 'companies most successful at creating long-term shareholder value build an organisational capability and institutionalise M&A processes ... they organise for opportunities' (2004). Having a competent, experienced person who is steeped in the Chinese way of doing things is a critical success factor.

The risk assessment process

In the risk assessment process, the steps are (1) identifying HR-related risks; (2) describing the risks; (3) assessing the risks in terms of likelihood versus impact; and (4) formulating migration plans in terms of timeliness and manageability. The steps for assessing HR Risks of an HR due diligence are depicted in Figure 5.1.

As a first step, probable and/or likely HR-related risks are identified, described and systematically grouped according to categories. Risk factors are evaluated using two factors: likelihood versus impact in the event that the identified risk should arise. The likelihood factor is represented on a 'weak to strong' continuum while the impact factor is determined

Figure 5.1   **Phases of HR risk assessments**

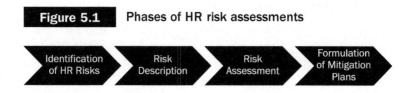

on a range from 'minimal to significant'. Figure 5.2 depicts the HR-related risk assessment matrix.

In order to assess HR-related risk, the risks are described and every single risk element that has been identified is plotted against each risk element. Table 5.1 illustrates how the risk assessment process is carried out. In this example, four risk items were deliberately chosen: residual value of state-assigned housing, translation risk, excessive headcount and a blatant flouting of state regulations. Against each of these identified risk items, a brief description of each risk is given. On the third column of the right-hand side of Table 5.1, risks are rated according to likelihood versus impact. A scenario is purposefully created such that each of the four risk items falls into each quadrant. This should provide an idea of what an effective risk assessment is and how it is carried out.

Figure 5.2   Likelihood versus impact assessment

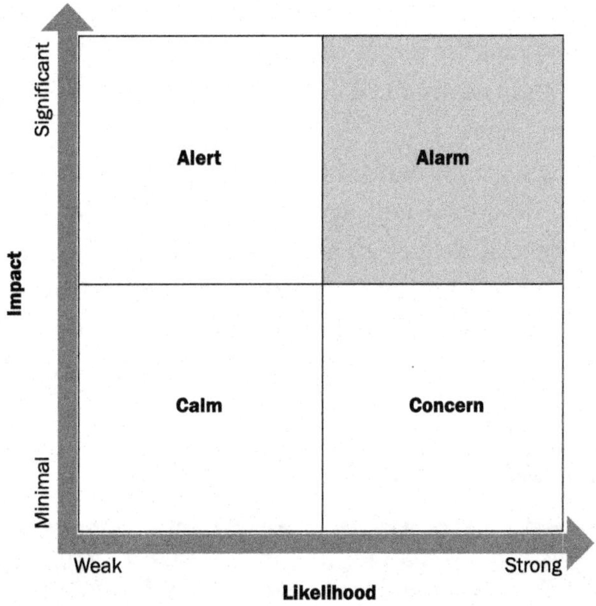

Table 5.1   Illustration of HR risk assessment

HR Risk	Description of Risk	Factor Rating	
		Likelihood	Impact
Residual value of state-assigned housing	Let us assume that this particular target SOE has been providing housing units to its burgeoning number of employees in its entire group. However, a preliminary indication is that for this target business unit, the percentage of employees enjoying this benefit is fewer than 8% and the last employee getting it was 4 years ago.	Obviously this will score highly as the practice is an established one. Rating = high	Since the % enjoying this benefit is low and the units are largely old, the rating will tend towards the low end. Rating = minimal
Translation risk	The assumption here is that the HR and Legal members of the Due Diligence team are both highly proficient (written and spoken) in the Chinese language and had done Due Diligence M&A projects in China in past years. They are steeped in Chinese culture and language nuances.	Rating = low	Rating = minimal
Excessive headcount	It is common knowledge that the headcount in Chinese SOEs normally is in multiples of those best-practice operating units in the more advanced industrialised countries. This can be taken virtually as a given. This being the case, there are also corresponding costs associated with it.	Rating = high	Rating = significant
Blatant flouting of state regulations	Assume that the JV is with a SOE. It is thus safe to adopt the view that being a SOE, it is most unlikely for it to flout state regulations.	Rating = low	Rating = significant

As a flow-through, the next step is to do a rating of the two variables, likelihood and impact. Having done this, the outcomes are transferred diagrammatically to the risk assessment matrix, as in Figure 5.2. As the scale increases from zero either horizontally towards the right or vertically towards the top, the degree of each factor increases in intensity, with the impact on the vertical axis and likelihood on the horizontal axis. The figure is divided into four quadrants, showing the upper right quadrant as being high on both likelihood and impact factors. This quadrant is labelled as Alarm; the upper left quadrant, being high on impact and low on likelihood, is labelled as Alert; the lower right quadrant, being high on likelihood but low on impact, is labelled as Concern; and the lower left quadrant, being low on both factors, is labelled as Calm.

This graphical depiction of risk assessment shows that all those risks that are confined to the Alarm quadrant require management attention, and mitigation plans must be formulated to address these risks as and when they arise. At the other extreme of the risk matrix, the risks that fall into the Calm bucket imply that these are relatively 'safe' areas and attention need not be paid to them. For the remaining two quadrants, stronger focus should be placed on Alert as the impact factor is critical. For the Concern quadrant, closer attention needs to be paid if the impact factor is assessed to be on the higher end, i.e. gravitating towards the Alarm quadrant. Figure 5.3 provides an example of the translation from the risks table into the risk matrix.

Residual value of state-assigned housing

(Assess as in Concern quadrant) Let us assume that for the purpose of this particular target the SOE has been providing housing units to the growing number of employees in its

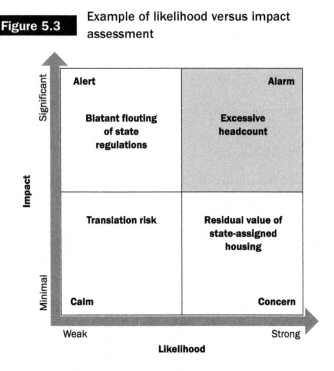

Figure 5.3   Example of likelihood versus impact assessment

group as a whole. However, a preliminary indication is that for this target business unit, the percentage of employees enjoying this benefit is less than 8 per cent and it is four years since the last employee received it.

Obviously this will score highly as the practice is an established one.

      Rating = minimal   Rating = high

Since the percentage enjoying this benefit is low and the units are largely old, the rating will tend towards the low end.

Translation risk

(Assess as in Calm quadrant) The assumption here is that the HR and legal department members of the due diligence team are both highly proficient (written and spoken) in the Chinese language and had previously conducted due diligence M&A projects in China. They are steeped in Chinese culture and language nuances.

Rating = low   Rating = minimal

Excessive headcount

(Assess as in Alarm quadrant) It is common knowledge that the headcount in Chinese SOEs is normally in multiples of those best-practice operating units in the more advanced industrialised countries. This can be taken virtually as a given. This being the case, there are also corresponding costs associated with it.

Rating = high   Rating = significant

Blatant flouting of state regulations

(Assess as in Alert quadrant) Assume that the JV is with a SOE. It is thus safe to adopt the view that, being a SOE, it is most unlikely that it will flout state regulations.

Rating = low   Rating = significant

Formulating mitigation plans

The final stage of the risk assessment process is the formulation of appropriate mitigation plans to specifically address those risks that are contained in the Alarm quadrant. Of the four risks that were identified, as indicated in Table 5.1, excessive headcount is situated in the Alarm quadrant. This risk carries a high rating for likelihood and impact. As discussed, this potential risk must be addressed by way of a plan to mitigate the impact of a fall-out. From a legal standpoint, the regulations dictate that all arrangements pertaining to the continued employment status of workers must be addressed before the authorities will proceed to approve the M&A deal. It is also recognised that the Chinese government is not inclined towards an immediate severance of employment for any unwanted workers, which may give rise to social unrest. At the same time, the actual situation could be such that these excess workers belong to a department which is an integral part of the business. As such, there is no justifiable basis for suggesting that the SOE absorbs them into their other lines of business as there might not be a match between worker profile and the business. In view of all this interplay of constraints, what then is the most equitable solution to counter this potential risk? In addressing this risk, one must ensure that the situation is clearly understood in its entirety. An excessive headcount issue is not a standalone case per se in the sense that there are additional corollary issues at play. The following questions may place the whole picture into its proper perspective.

- Following this particular M&A deal, will there be follow-on deals in the near future with the same SOE within close proximity to the present locality? If the answer is a resounding 'yes', then there is the need to explore whether this excessive headcount can be absorbed into future deals.

- What is the specific number of excess headcount we are dealing with? What is the excess as a ratio of total headcount? This needs to be determined and verified in the course of the due diligence.

- Should there be a tacit agreement with the Chinese party to reduce the headcount by retrenchment at some future point, the vital question arising would be the service portion relating to those earlier years which were spent in contributing to the SOE business.

- An extended issue relating to the recognition of years of service with the SOE is whether this could be resolved by computing the quantum payable at the point of the M&A deal being finalised. This means that the retrenchment compensation for the period of employment with the SOE is computed on present terms and frozen at that material point in time. But one question still remains: must this quantum be paid to the workers before the transfer to the newly formed JV is made effective?

- With the retrenchment compensation being computed, regardless of whether it is paid out at the point of transfer or set aside as an accounting provision, does this therefore lead to the conclusion that the new date of joining will be in accordance with the date of transfer into the newly formed company?

- What kind of ramifications will this issue create when it comes to the management integration phase?

These questions highlight the fact that frequently a risk item is not a standalone issue. Owing to the relatedness of interconnected issues at the workplace, the case can be intensely complicated and/or complex. The ultimate decision is to determine if a chosen mitigation plan is adequate to address the risk it entails. To determine the adequacy of a mitigation plan, additional factors must be taken into account. The factors are manageability and timeliness. Manageability measures the degree of difficulty of managing the risk at hand and timeliness looks into how quickly the risk can be resolved as soon as it appears.

Figure 5.4 depicts an assessment matrix to determine the feasibility of the mitigation plan of a defined risk. As in the

Figure 5.4 Manageability vs Timeliness mitigation assessment plan

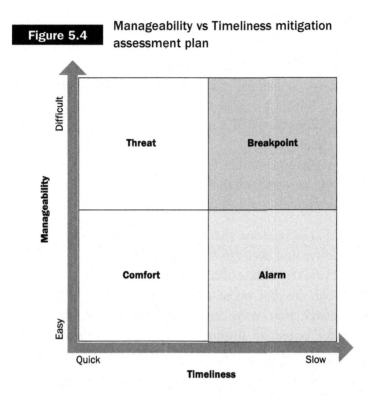

case of the risk assessment matrix, the mitigation plan matrix is divided into four quadrants, with manageability on the vertical axis and timeliness on the horizontal axis. As we navigate from base zero at the origin upwards along the vertical axis, the degree of difficulty increases for manageability. As we navigate towards the right side of the horizontal axis, the response time needed to resolve the risk is less. As in Likelihood/Impact illustrated in Figure 5.2, the quadrant which gives rise to concern is in the upper right-hand corner, labelled as Breakpoint. Any risk within the Threat quadrant must also be treated with caution and utmost care as the degree of managing the risk may be fraught with difficulties. Needless to say, those risks falling into the Comfort quadrant are the ones of least concern. In the event of a high-rated risk appearing with a high degree of difficulty in manageability coupled with a slow response in timeliness, the issue can only be addressed through a business consideration. In other words, the one overwhelming consideration is whether this becomes a deal-breaking issue.

One working solution that could be considered is to arrive at an agreement based on initial principles. The initial principles take into account the following:

- A mutual recognition that excessive headcount is counter-productive and needs to be addressed over time (say three to five years from date of commencement of JV operations). Although the time taken seems long, the comfort is in the knowledge that it is formally documented, thus pre-empting potential disputes or strong objections from arising in the future.

- Following a 'transition' period of two-three years, for example, downsizing of excessive headcount would commence.

- The yardstick to be applied to determine the 'downsized' employees must be agreed to avoid future conflicts. In this situation, one should be mentally prepared for extraneous consideration to be given to exceptional cases which are frequently linked to connections or *guānxi* in the Chinese context.

- The downsizing exercise may be done in stages over an extended period depending on the severity of the excess. If the number of 'downsized' employees as a percentage of total headcount is high, more than one retrenchment exercise may be planned to reduce the social unrest and anti-government demonstrations.

Negotiation guidelines

It is good practice, at the outset, to establish a common understanding on the boundary markers that would apply to all parties on negotiations. This will preclude misunderstanding, which can prevent an amiable relationship from being built and, worse still, develop into distrust and disrespect. Such markers would include authority to decide, points of agreement arising from negotiations, legality of furnished documents and items to be or not to be included in the final M&A agreement.

Negotiating parties

It is a practice that simultaneous negotiations can take place among different functional groups, i.e. finance, operations (likely to incorporate safety, health and environment), HR and business (which will take care of the overall core terms). The advantage of so doing is to save time and resources so that the various domain experts can discuss and resolve areas of conflicts on specific subject-matter in a focused environment. The composition of each of these functional groups is not critical and can be left to the discretion of each M&A party. What is critical for the HR negotiations group is an understanding for the negotiating leader to be given the authority to decide and agree. What this amounts to is that once an agreement is reached after due negotiations, then it is binding on both parties. The paramount reason for having this understanding is that neither party to the negotiation process should turn around with the stand that the negotiating leader does not have the authority to make a certain decision at a subsequent stage. Once this happens, things can get messy as items of agreement could have been 'horse-traded', especially if these verge on deal-breaking issues. So how does one go backwards and yet maintain a level playing field?

Points of agreement

Basic issues to resolve before the commencement of negotiations would be the language to use for transcribing the points that have been agreed upon, the party responsible for transcribing these points and formalisation of these points of agreement. Since Chinese regulations recognise only Hanyu as the official language for M&A agreements, it would make good sense and be consistent that Hanyu be used as the language for these transcripts. This will also facilitate the incorporation of those items which are intended to form a part of the M&A agreement. Identifying the party to transcribe the points is not as critical as the process by which the transcripts would be formalised. The way we favour using is for both parties to recognise that the points of agreement are taken in good order by signifying mutual acceptance with both the leaders of the negotiating parties signing the transcripts and with copies being kept by both parties. It should also be mutually agreed that the signed transcripts would remain binding on both parties notwithstanding the fact that some of the agreed items may not eventually be incorporated into the M&A agreement, whether in full or in part. We hold the view that minutes of meetings, if deemed necessary to be taken, are only intended as records for the purpose of referral to gain an insight as to how each point was discussed, argued and finally agreed. The critical need is for every single point that had been agreed upon to be formalised at the end of each meeting. This will provide the legal platform for the final M&A agreement to be drafted and for the legal team to consider the specific items that will form the scope of the agreement.

Those items which are considered to fall outside the agreement are not considered non-binding, and remain valid for compliance purposes.

Furnished documents/information

Any documents which are requested during the due diligence study phase are to be treated as valid, and information contained therein should be understood to be official and accurate. It is therefore useful that when information or documents are requested, the date of validity be stipulated to prevent misunderstanding and dispute. Furthermore, every document that is provided by any one party must rightfully carry the signature of the negotiating leader. This serves to confirm the source of the document. For the purpose of good control and coordination, it is best that a single control point for documents, information, queries or request flow be agreed upon. This will eliminate confusion and conflicts over authoritative source of document supply.

M&A agreement

It is only to be expected that the drafting of the M&A agreement would fall within the purview of the legal team in any M&A exercise. However, this does not mean that other functional teams would have no input or influence over what items need to be incorporated into the agreement. In fact, it is equally to be expected that for HR matters, the HR team should be in a position to influence the specific clauses or items to be included. On top of this, the HR team should play the role of ensuring that the various provisions or conditions or constraints are appropriately and comprehensively captured in their essence and spirit. This is an important step towards minimising potential issues from arising out of misunderstanding or misinterpretation over what had been discussed during the negotiations phase and supposedly agreed upon and minuted.

HR strategy for a merger in China

Before one enters into a merger in China, it is imperative that one understands the specific nature of the merger that one is going in for. By definition, a merger is the joining together of two or more companies through a mutual agreement that is arrived at pursuant to relevant provisions of the appropriate company law. For the purpose of this book, we are not concerned with the manner by which the transaction is financially or legally structured. Our focus is to examine only the HR ramifications of the deal. Notwithstanding this, it is pertinent to point out that in the context of China, a merger can only occur between two Chinese business entities. It is interesting to note that currently there are no regulations prohibiting the merger between a Chinese entity and a foreign entity. Our aim is to delve into the question of management control. In this section, we would assume that the foreign party would have at least an equal say, if not full management control of the JV, without which there is no management issue to even talk about. Once the management control issue is settled, then broadly speaking, we can proceed to categorise them under six scenarios in so far as an HR perspective of looking at mergers goes. The rationale for taking such an approach stems from the fact that HR management fundamentally looks at people-related issues, systems, processes and policies. The underlying assumption here is that the more complex an organisation is and the higher the headcount figure, the greater and more meticulous will be the need to adopt an appropriate HR strategy. Our observation is that many foreign multinational corporations look only at the financial costs (which obviously include HR-related costs) and frequently ignore the headcount impact. Being HR practitioners, besides payroll and related expenses, we look at one other factor. This relates to productivity and work processes/systems. Many of the processes in China's state-owned sector have created badly ingrained habits. What made it worse is that these habits which have been left uncorrected over working decades have been transformed into acceptable ways of doing things. This is one counter-productive trait that must be corrected, even if it means working painfully slowly. It is from this angle that we contend that counter-productive habits can be more costly in the longer run than direct HR costs, and companies need to study this implication as part of their HR due diligence efforts.

Let us now describe the scenarios that one will likely be confronted with when entering into a merger situation in China. We are by no means trying to suggest here that these six scenarios are exhaustive; there are certainly other possible permutations that may arise, which we believe would not create a significant impact on the HR strategy to be adopted as these will most probably be a variation to any one of the six scenarios outlined here.

Scenario 1

In this situation, the Chinese party will inject land, machines/equipment, buildings (which we will broadly term 'assets') and people into the JV while the foreign partner injects capital (see Figure 5.5). The biggest headache for the HR practitioner here would be a case of excessive staffing, where the Chinese M&A regulatory authorities will not approve any immediate downsizing. And for most foreign corporations which are so attuned to best-practice operating standards, such a situation cannot be allowed to fester in perpetuity. What solution can HR offer here?

Figure 5.5   Scenario 1

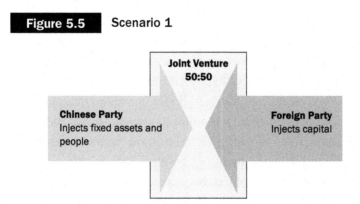

HR strategy

In addressing this situation, the focus is on staffing levels, contractual obligations/terms and conditions, HR practices, processes and systems, payroll and related expenses, statutory costs and unseen HR costs.

Scenario 2

In this instance, the Chinese side desires to split the JV into phases where the Chinese will inject assets and people in the first phase and additional assets and people in a later phase, whereas the foreign party injects capital for both phases (see Figure 5.6). There are two probable rationales for the Chinese side to adopt such a JV strategy. The first is that the Chinese partner is using this as a negotiation ploy by dangling a bigger potential carrot further down the road if results of the JV prove acceptable. Results as used here are not necessarily confined to the financial aspect, but, probably more critically, to a partnership relationship. The second is that therein lies an indication of their feeling of uncertainty in dealing with the chosen foreign party and they are therefore introducing a transitional phase into the JV equation to assess the compatibility of the JV relationship.

Figure 5.6   Scenario 2

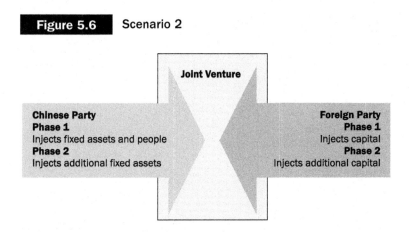

HR strategy

Confronted with such a situation, the HR strategy, besides focusing on those areas outlined in Scenario 1, will have two other aspects to look into. One is the overriding phase 2 business consideration which cannot be ignored. And the other is the details pertaining to the phase 2 people assets. The litmus test lies in examining how far or how much the HR factor differs between the two sets of people belonging to the different business units that are to be injected into the JV in the longer run. The underlying success factor here is whether the Chinese will open their books to be examined by you. This may turn out to be a stumbling block which the Chinese side has no obligation to provide since the phase 2 assets and people do not fall within the ambit of phase 1 JV negotiations. Can a case be justifiably made for access to information that falls outside the purview of present discussions?

Scenario 3

This is a situation whereby both parties inject assets as well as people into the JV which are likely to be in unequal

Figure 5.7   Scenario 3

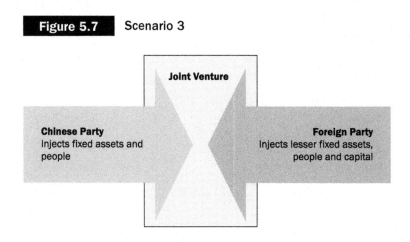

proportion and the levelling is done via capital injection by the party with the lesser assets (see Figure 5.7).

HR strategy

In this particular scenario, the sensitivity and degree of complexity lie in the differences in terms and conditions and benefits that are being enjoyed by the two sets of people. While the foreign party employees are likely to earn a higher wage, the same cannot be said of benefits-in-kind. Therein lies the complexity of finding an equitable methodology of levelling the employment terms without causing a burdensome increase in wage and related costs.

Scenario 4

This scenario is again characterised by agreeing to a two-phase approach to forming the JV; with both agreeing that phase 1 is a greenfield project and then plan for phase 2 to be a brownfield one where the Chinese party will inject assets and people and the foreign party injects capital in both phases (see Figure 5.8).

Figure 5.8   Scenario 4

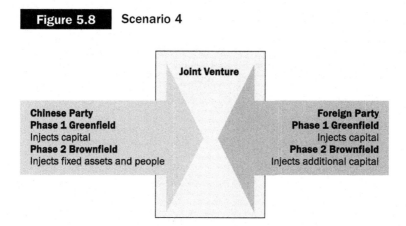

HR strategy

The strategic advantage arising from such a scenario is that the JV management (which is assumed to be either being ceded to the foreign party or at least the foreign party having an equal say) can dictate terms and conditions on a clean slate since the JV kicks off its business on a greenfield platform. However, the singular constraint to this situation is that in deciding its HR policies, processes and procedures, it has to take into consideration the prevailing situation in the Chinese business unit that is planned for injection into the JV at some future time.

Scenario 5

This situation is akin to Scenario 1 in only one aspect; that is, the Chinese party injects assets and the foreign party injects capital (see Figure 5.9). The vital difference is that the people who are needed to manage and operate the business are on loan from the Chinese party through an employee loan agreement. This means that the JV is being managed without any people being legally employed by it. The

Figure 5.9   Scenario 5

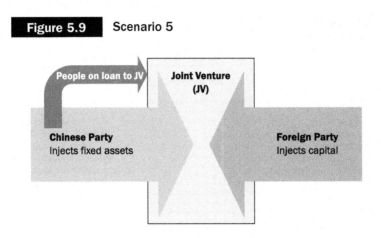

HR issues in this scenario would relate to the way these people are handled and managed while they are working in the premises of the JV, which are likely to be physically the same building they have been working in while continuing to be under the legal employment of the Chinese party. Examples of HR-related issues in such a type of employee loan arrangement would be right of 'hire and fire', leave administration, unauthorised absences, latecoming, redeployment, expenses arising from skills upgrading through training, payroll administration, worker injuries in the course of work, company rules and regulations which differ from the Chinese party, etc. The overriding factor certainly lies in the overall fees to be levied by the Chinese party from whom these personnel are lent. What is the equitable and acceptable method of computation to be used?

HR strategy

This case looks deceptively simple in that there is no 'employee' to deal with and thus HR would have no role to play. However, we would contend that the same rigour be applied when one undertakes an HR Due Diligence exercise in order to be aware of implications and pitfalls when negotiating for the employee loan agreement. The complication for HR would be a situation where the decision taken and agreed by both Chinese and foreign parties is that not all existing employees from the Chinese party will be absorbed or loaned by the JV. The vital question is how one is to determine who are the suitable employees to be loaned. There is thus the need for HR to think of a system or methodology to identify these staff. And one cannot rule out the possibility that there could be objections from the Chinese party on the grounds that the method to be used is seen as unfair to the employees.

One of the book's authors, in carrying out an HR Due Diligence on a privately owned enterprise in Beijing, discovered that the particular business unit's statutory contributions were significantly lower than would have been expected had due compliance been observed. What this means is that the particular business unit had been under-declaring the wage levels to minimise their statutory obligations to the state and employees. If this practice was not immediately rectified at the actual time of merger, but subsequently discovered, it would certainly lead to disastrous consequences for the foreign party. On the other hand, even if the foreign party so desires to rectify the situation, there are practical difficulties that may be encountered as well. For one, if the payroll administration for this on-loan group of employees continues to be undertaken by the Chinese party, then this wrongful practice may continue or be resorted to at some point without the foreign party being any the wiser. This is a plausible scenario as the vast majority of these people are 'migrant' workers and it is common for them to work in apparent silence in the urban centres under such unfair conditions. However, one cannot dismiss the possibility that a case of unfair treatment may be lodged with the arbitration centres upon termination of contract of these people. The issue of which party to lodge this case against very much rests with the employee. He may opt to lodge the complaint against both parties as he can rightfully claim that he has worked for both under differing terms and conditions, notwithstanding the fact that he is legally employed by the Chinese party. The fact that a complaint of unfair treatment is lodged, justly or wrongfully, will lead to an investigation by the authorities concerned. This is one implication that can arise from such a JV arrangement.

Scenario 6

The main feature of this scenario is that both parties inject capital into a greenfield JV and future business expansion plans are treated as organic growth and personnel needs are filled from external sources. In this scenario, there are no internal staff resources to grapple with from the onset of the setting up of the JV (see Figure 5.10).

Figure 5.10   Scenario 6

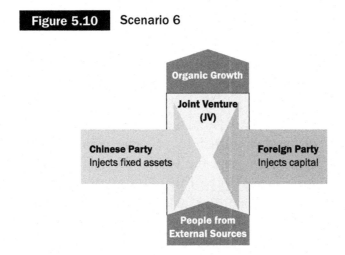

HR strategy

In this instance, the HR role is the most straightforward since there are no HR implications to look into for the moment or the future. It will be simply a case of determining the appropriate systems to put in place once the JV starts its business operations.

General HR strategy

Notwithstanding whatever scenarios one is faced with, there are two common areas which HR practitioners undertaking HR due diligence for an M&A exercise in China need to grapple with. From the point where an M&A target is identified by the business folks, it is imperative that HR understands whether there are any unwanted departments or functions or sections of the business. Knowing that there are indeed departments of functions that do not quite fit into the business plan, the obvious question that follows would be deciding and agreeing with the Chinese party as to what to do with the people who belong to this area. Secondly, there is also the need to address any issue of over-staffing within the target business unit. At this juncture, HR practitioners must be aware that legally speaking, parties to a merger in China must make arrangements to ensure the employment status of the original employees of the entity being merged is not compromised. Without such an arrangement for workers' employment status being satisfactorily settled, official approval for the merger is likely to be withheld. It is worth noting that a process of formal consultation with workers is recognised by the authorities. Although one can argue here that the responsibility of this worker settlement issue rests with the target entity, one must also take into account the fact that any mishandling or poor handling of this issue may impact the progress status of the transaction.

The spectre of workers having unrealistic or unjustified expectations of additional benefits or compensation is always hanging in the balance.

What about an acquisition?

In the case of an acquisition, there is no JV partner to contend with in the first instance. This will provide the full freedom to act and put systems into place at will as long as these do not infringe upon prevailing regulations and as long as there are no agreed constraints being imposed by way of the acquisition agreement. For example, if the acquisition agreement provides for a stipulation of no retrenchment for a given number of years from date of takeover, then a situation of over-staffing cannot be resolved through retrenchment and alternative means would have to be looked at. Notwithstanding the leeway that one has in a situation of an acquisition, there is the need to address the question of integrating the newly acquired business unit into the group practice. At what level is the integration to be achieved, in-country or regional or global? Will the integration be confined to HR systems and processes only or would it extend to cultural and value assimilation? This subject of integration will be covered in detail in Chapter 6.

Deal-breaking and deal-making issues

During the initial preparation phase as discussed in Chapter 3, the HR due diligence team member should get acquainted with what the deal-breaking issues are. This does not, in any way, suggest that such issues are 'untouchables', but rather should be put to strategic leverage against one's own desired gains. Deal-breakers are essentially areas where these form 'must give-aways'. What if these deal-breakers are also HR's desired 'haves'? Herein lies a business decision. If it is truly a deal-breaker, then what it means is that there is a conflict of interests and if these cannot be 'give-aways' it only means that there is no deal to start with. From a business standpoint, if the deal is a must-have, then HR's interests would have to be compromised. Therein lies the essence for HR to be aware of deal-breakers. A common example that one is likely to experience is that at the start of the JV or WOFE, the Chinese side would extract a commitment that there would be no retrenchment of employees, despite potential excessive over-staffing. Does such a commitment mean that it is given in perpetuity? The answer is an obvious 'no'. A commitment of this nature should also be accompanied by a pre-agreed timeline; after which, should the surplus situation persist, then a downsizing exercise would be carried out.

Concluding the deal and signing the agreement

Appropriately armed with the knowledge of which are the issues that make or break the deal and having deliberated and decided upon the most optimal HR strategy to adopt, one then enters into the negotiations brimming with confidence. Once the negotiations waterway is smoothly steered through, there comes the crucial part of preparing for the signing of the M&A agreement. This activity is normally led by the legal team. The principal role that HR plays in this particular area is to ensure that the various provisions that had been discussed, negotiated and ultimately agreed upon are accurately captured in meaning, nuances and definition. In the event of a legal wrangle, it is the Chinese-worded version that counts, and it is necessary to stress once again that extreme care must be taken to ensure that what had been translated into the Hanyu language is accurately done. Whatever items or provisions that are not included into this main agreement can always be mutually agreed for inclusion (meaning with legal obligations for mutual compliance) in a separate document. One fine detail to delve into here is that there is a time-gap between the date of signing the agreement and the date of enforcement or date of handing/ taking over. Besides the question of inventory and assets listing (which are outside the purview of HR), HR will similarly have its own share of items and listing to take care of. Prudence and care need to be exercised. Finally, there will be systems (software systems especially) that require continuity. Examples of this are the payroll and HR information systems. Once things are deemed to be handed over, all responsibilities may terminate. Certain obligations need to continue beyond the takeover event.

6

Managing integration

Abstract: Integrating individual businesses from distinct national and organisation cultures and diverse ethnicity is a challenge. The issues confronting management integration depends on the strength of the affective relationships of the parties; the comprehensiveness and thoroughness in conducting HR due diligence; the assessments to uncover unseen risks; and the resolution of disputes in negotiations. The handing and taking over processes focus on the HR infrastructure, organisational and cultural integration, and the retention of talented employees.

Key words: cultural integration, organisational integration, structural integration, corporate values, ethnicity, dispute resolution, talent retention

Ties that bind

In a recent M&A study conducted by Mercer on China, it was reported that the human resource issues are managing organisational cultural integration; retaining, focusing and attracting talent; and maintaining relationships after the deal is done. While building an affective relationship focuses on conducting HR due diligence to uncover unseen costs, maintaining the relationship after the deal is completed requires management to integrate individual work processes into the newly formed joint venture or a wholly-owned foreign enterprise. More importantly, management integration involves aligning and harmonising people and processes to achieve organisational performance.

The signing of the M&A agreement signifies the completion of the due diligence process and the culmination of intensive negotiations between the foreign organisations and the Chinese parties. At the same time, it marks the beginning of a transfer of management to the newly formed joint venture or a wholly owned foreign enterprise. What does a management transfer entail? In managing the transfer, the management integration plan must incorporate the formation of a management team, that is, the team that is responsible and accountable for taking over the management of the business unit which is either a joint venture or a wholly-owned foreign enterprise. Central to this plan is the appointment of the general manager of the business unit. In the case of a JV, this is predicated on the assumption that the agreement is to appoint the foreign partner to manage the business. Apart from the general manager position, there are the appointments of heads of departments. Which are the functions that are considered to be critical to the success of the business? Typically, the finance and operations portfolios are key areas to be managed by the foreign partners. Business processes, systems and procedures are guided by international standards and the Chinese may not have the expertise, relevant work experience, or exposure to manage the portfolios.

Handing/taking over process

The handing/taking over process covers various aspects: physical assets, people assets, information and systems. The physical assets would normally be within the purview of the financial due diligence team. HR is responsible for its people assets. These assets may be categorised as:

- **HR *policies and systems***
  - Items include payroll, HR information systems, HR manuals, employee handbook, employee personal files.
- **HR *processes***
  - These cover resourcing as in recruitment and selection, performance management, compensation and benefits management, training and development, staff planning and budgeting.
- **HR *information***
  - Work- or performance-related – this deals with shift schedules, overtime work, payroll, all forms of allowances, appraisals and bonus payments.
  - Discipline-related – these records cover punctuality, absence and behavioural issues.
  - Benefits-related – these records include all forms of leave, reimbursement claims and payment eligibility.

Prior to taking over the management of the newly formed joint venture or a wholly-owned foreign enterprise, it is important to obtain an assurance that there are no outstanding payments owing to employees; such claims may be unpleasant and time-consuming as they become a financial liability. A timeline must be agreed where all claims for reimbursements or payments are settled by a mutually agreed date. Thereafter, no further claims will be allowed. Notwithstanding the fact that future claims are of no concern to the new business entity, the case remains that claims will turn into employees' grievances which require time and attention to resolve.

HR administration

An employee's employment status with the Chinese party must be effectively dealt with before the person can be considered to be transferred to the new company. On the one hand, the employee's status with the SOE must be effectively terminated and on the other hand a new employment relationship must be forged with the new business unit (be it a JV or a WOFE). A key employment term that needs attention is the recognition of the length of service with the SOE prior to the formation of the new business unit. If the service is not recognised and where a commensurate compensation has been agreed upon between the parties to the M&A deal, the party which is benefitting from this compensation must be explicitly stipulated. If the beneficiary party is the employees, the question of disbursement must also be agreed upon and stipulated. Details of computation methodology to determine the amount of computation and a schedule of payment must be included and communicated. Extensive speculation on incorrect and misleading information that is continuously being circulated in the factory or office premises may cause disquiet among employees. Open communications will serve to ensure that transparency, reasonableness and fairness are seen to be at play and avoid raising suspicion that any group of employees are being favoured or have gained unduly at the expense of another group of employees. Over the years, demonstrations at government offices have been known to be held, even in third tier cities. In the last two decades of China's accelerated economic growth, two trends had emerged. The first was the large influx of migrant workers from the provinces into the urban centres. The second was that increasingly over time, workers have become acutely aware of their employment rights and are willing to stand up for their rights if these are seen to be compromised or abused.

Organisational integration

We learned in the earlier chapters that successful M&A transactions are very much predicated upon the acquiring companies building an experienced corporate team, with the expertise to pursue M&A opportunities, and who are intimately involved in all stages of M&A activities until the business is successfully transferred to the newly formed business. The key activity to conclude the M&A transaction as a whole is for the business to arrive at a steady state of its operation. Studies have consistently shown that more than half of M&As fail to meet purchaser objectives because of a deficiency in management integration and in standard structural and cultural fit. To reach an operational steady state, the newly formed business (JV or WOFE) must be organisationally integrated to align to every aspect of the business. In almost every published survey that tracks M&A failure in terms of total shareholder return, cultural integration is consistently at the top of the list of priorities.

Structural integration

Organisational structure

At the primary level, consideration ought to be given to the organisational structure. How integrated is the organisation at the country or national level? If the corporation has an existing country organisation in China, the issue may be to merge this new business entity into the structure. For an acquisition, the integration can be relatively straightforward, but in the case of a JV, an affective relationship with the Chinese partner needs to be factored into the management integration process.

Job grade structure

As soon as a new entity is formed from a JV or WOFE, the issue of an integrated job and grading structure needs to be addressed. At the country level, it is necessary to determine if the integration of job grades is necessary. Regardless of the decision on the integration or non-integration of job grades, there are implications that may or may not have financial consequences. An integration of job grades will facilitate transfer of employees between business units. Without job grade integration, it may still be possible to legally transfer employees between business units. One plausible way is to second an employee from Company A to Company B for a stipulated period of time, with all the terms and conditions of Company A whilst the employee is physically working in Company B.

Salary structure

This is a more complex issue than the integration of job grading structure. In the first instance, salaries differ significantly between first, second, and third tier cities in China. Hence, it may be justifiable to have different salary structures across regions. Even so, salary structures that are respectively applicable to cities, municipalities or provinces within China do not address the problem of salaries in all instances. Problems arise when the acquired company or JV unit is located in a precinct where the group has other operating units, especially when they are all in similar industrial segments. In a matter of time, comparisons of salaries and wages will be made and dissensions will surface. If the new entity is a JV, it is a totally different business unit and is independently managed, with a board that has no accountability to the corporate management of the foreign party. Hence, employees may accept the disparity in salaries and structures. However, if the new entity is a WOFE, the issue is more complex as the cost structure may make it financially more viable to subsume the new unit into a single organisational structure. This would imply that employees from the SOE would be fully absorbed into the foreign entity.

Benefits structure

The key driver for the coordination of employment benefits is the issue of standardisation. Is it necessary for employee benefits to be coordinated and standardised across the country, let alone the city or province? Invariably, there are advantages and disadvantages for pursuing options in standardisation or localisation. Although a standardised set of benefits may facilitate employee transfers, it does not necessarily mean that a non-standardised set will impede transfers. As transfers from one business entity to another require the tacit consent of the employee, a solution is to offer an attractive total remuneration package. Total remuneration for transferred employees would certainly require them to swap specific existing compensable items with other items that may be perceived by employees as non-beneficial.

It is important to remember that an existing benefit item should not be taken away until it has been offset against other compensable items. For each compensable item, there is a corresponding cost attached. In the case of a swap: where

Company A has benefit X and Company B has benefit Y (assuming benefits X and Y are of equal value), using one item to offset against another would be perceived as reasonable. In reality, benefit items would always have unequal perceived value, from the organisational as well as the employee perspective. A possible solution is to group benefit items into 'baskets' of perceived equal value, making the options of swapping compensable items more palatable. For the moment, flexible benefit schemes, as practised in Westernised economies, are not made available in the organisations studied.

Cultural integration

Corporate values

Employees' behaviour is largely driven by the company's code of conduct, ethical standards and policies. Underlying all these is the set of corporate values that the management promulgates to its employees. Corporate values are by no means locally dictated or driven. A global initiative is needed. No matter where the company is operating, this set of values does not differ from one geographical boundary to another. The meaning, essence and norms are similar, notwithstanding the fact that a given behaviour can be found to be widespread or even acceptable in a specific location or country. For example, a company which embraces integrity as a corporate value will not accept giving kickbacks to potential vendors or clients, even though the environment in which it operates is one where such practices are customary and commonplace. Lovallo et al. (2007) argue that 'unanticipated cultural conflicts are well known to cause merger problems; less well known is the idea that conflict can arise even in the most anodyne situations'.

Our experience in China has taught us an important and invaluable lesson. To change people's habits, it is more effective to carry out initiatives right at the onset of taking over the business. To instil corporate values, two elements must prevail. The first is that the same dedicated team infuses the same message relentlessly from top management to the lowest level on the shop-floor. This will ensure consistency in message and its meaning. Secondly, each stipulated value must be accompanied by detailed explanations as to what specific elements constitute this value. Moreover, concrete instances are provided to capture the true essence of every value. An example that can be used to illustrate this is taking the value of 'collaboration' or 'teamwork'. It is easy to understand what this word means in English. But to define it as a value of a new culture, then translate the value into specific expectations of behaviour and an actionable word is a different matter altogether. One may like to use an example of a group of employees at work where one of the members is seen to be mired in an unknown problem. As a fellow team member, how does one react to such an incident? Does one adopt the attitude that since the fellow-worker does not call for help, one just goes about one's own work and lets matters rest as they are? Or does one voluntarily extend a hand outwards and ask if you can be of help? Collaboration dictates that one extends one's hand to help.

Values are merely statements of intent. Examples help to translate these statements into action plans. This gives clarity of purpose. Perhaps it may be useful to align the Westernised version of behavioural anchor rating scales (BARS) to the Chinese context. As in most instances, it is more difficult to unlearn and relearn work habits and practices than to learn those behaviours properly in the first place.

In driving values down the organisational chain, two intervention tools are useful. The first is to develop an effective communications plan and the second is to rely on change management to overcome undue resistance or negative perceptions or sheer inertia towards proposed changes.

Behavioural standards

Standards may be easily defined where the items are objectively quantifiable. Examples of standards that may be measured objectively include distance, flow rate, weight, height, speed, brightness. It is often difficult to quantify and measure behaviours in an objective manner. Behaviour can be visible, but in many instances it may be difficult to measure. Although organisations may place a behaviour anchor in terms of work performance, it is still difficult to define a specific behaviour to be 'notches' above or below tolerance level and deemed as acceptable behaviour. How then does one determine if behaviour is acceptable or unacceptable? Many companies adopt a defined code of ethics or conduct, and a long list of bad behaviours that constitute misconduct. Regardless, the acid test of what constitutes unacceptable behaviour depends on whether such conduct is challenged in a court of law. Will the case stand up to arbitration scrutiny if the notions of *QingFaLi*, as discussed in Chapter 2, are applied to interpret what is otherwise deemed unacceptable behaviour?

There are two vital parameters in determining an acceptable standard of behaviour. One is to use either the societal norm or entrenched way of behaving in the given environment. For example, it is not illegal for male workers to wear shorts to work; nevertheless the normal dress code in the company is to wear long trousers. Thus it can reasonably be argued that the wearing of shorts to work is unacceptable, perhaps due to occupational health and safety concerns, even if it does not infringe state laws or regulations. The second point to adhere to is exemplary conduct of senior employees. It was asserted in a Manpower white paper that companies cannot just 'talk the talk'; they have to live and breathe those (desired corporate) values. In addition, it is reported that leaders need to embody the values in their actions every day. Senior employees are obliged to lead by example. It has often been said that one must not just be correct but be seen to be correct. Negative examples will inevitably be imitated and, over time, be seen as being accepted.

Institutionalised habits

In the context of our book, we have used this term to mean behaviour which has been ingrained over time, being treated as acceptable and where both managers and employees view such behaviour as in conformity to standards. Where such habit runs against the grain of acceptable norms, it must be quickly eradicated. An example that we have come across was that in a volatile chemical industry where the products are of an incendiary and explosive nature. The employee handbook states that an employee caught smoking in the company's premises will be subject to a warning in the first instance and to termination of contract for repeated misconduct. However, in the foreign party's safety standards globally, any employee (regardless of seniority in grade or years of service) caught smoking will be summarily dismissed from service. In this situation, a conflict exists between global and local standards of acceptable behaviour. In terms of the foreign entity's safety standard, smoking is unthinkable and is a serious breach of conduct. The nature of the industry is such that an accident due to smoking can potentially cause serious injuries or even death. Hence, allowing smoking on its premises is considered a breach of safety standards and must not be condoned. In a nation of smokers, the Chinese may accept smoking as part of their way of life. However, the severe consequences of smoking in a highly inflammable and combustible work environment necessitates that smoking is eradicated immediately and without compromise. Perhaps this example is rather extreme and there will be many instances whereby change is necessary but the impact, if change is not implemented, is perhaps less severe. The difficulty is to make a case for changing those habits which do not appear to be of high risk or severe costs impact. It is always so easy to 'let sleeping dogs lie' or avoid 'rocking the boat'. However, the risk of being badly bitten by the same sleeping dogs at some future point cannot be ruled out; and the consequences can be regrettably painful. Whether a given habit should be quickly eradicated depends on the degree to which such a habit impacts upon the core values of the organisation.

Cultivating relationships

In the preparation phase for the due diligence, the fundamental objective of having a JV or a WOFE would have been addressed. If the outcome is a JV, this leads to further strategising, that is, the composition of the negotiations team. The core in building an organisational capability lies in this negotiations team. Will it be a global team which specialises in all M&A deals to be undertaken, or will it draw on China-based expertise? It is worth recalling that China is not at all homogeneous; fragmented by diverse dialect groups that are mutually unintelligible, customs, ethnicity, level of economic development and disparate living standards. Jacques (2009) describes China as a 'civilization state' and contends that China's provinces are far more differentiated than Europe's nation-states, including Eastern Europe and the Balkans. Dealing with such cultural complexity and diversity, it may be beneficial to have a singularly focused in-country team.

When two teams of divergent backgrounds meet and negotiate over a protracted duration that stretches into two or three years, a certain level of shared understanding and relationship is inevitable. It is common for some of the negotiations to continue over dinners and drinks. In such a social setting, where the tension of negotiations (which can be adversarial) is removed, small talk can go a long way towards building up a relationship of understanding, trust and empathy. Can this relationship be further strengthened and leveraged upon going into the future? This, of course, is predicated upon the assumption that a JV is successfully and finally concluded. In order for this relationship that is newly gained, forged and strengthened to develop further, the foreign party should define at the outset the roles members of the negotiation team adopt as soon as the JV is formed. This relationship will be an asset when JV issues arise in the future.

To underline the importance of building up a relationship with the Chinese partner, the financial value of relationships between company personnel and important external stakeholders, unlike the value of tangible assets, is easy to overlook because relationship value cannot be quantified through traditional analysis. Building affective relations with customers, suppliers and government authorities is often critical to M&A success. More importantly, affective relationships should be built with the Chinese partner in the first instance.

Managing expectations

As soon as a target company is identified for potential merger or acquisition and the process of due diligence is put in place, information will inevitably and quickly be circulated to the general workforce. Just as swiftly as the news of M&A spreads, rising expectations of a better tomorrow will be anticipated, especially if the intended partner is a foreign entity. One source which will lend credence to such perception is the change in behaviour of the management team as they are privy to such information. If a senior member of the management team starts to develop ungrounded expectations of a better future coupled with changes in habits, employees may interpret such behaviour as confirmation of an intending M&A with foreign partners, and hence a better future. Quick acceptance of the veracity of M&A prevails and subsequent actions to contain rumours and speculations will be met with disbelief and negative responses from the employees. It is thus critical for the HR due diligence team to be sensitive to the grapevine and to move swiftly to quash speculation of intending M&A transactions. One effective way to address speculative risk is at the negotiations phase. Confidentiality of any discussion pertaining to M&A must be maintained and a commitment must be gained from the Chinese that senior management will not communicate information on the planned merger or acquisition to the workforce. However, there will be unavoidable speculation on a potential deal as soon as negotiations commence. Therefore, the Chinese party may appoint an official spokesperson for the M&A exercise, to whom any queries by employees can be centrally directed for responses. This will serve to minimise distorted information or half-truths circulating among employees.

Improving processes/revamping systems

A key driver for achieving efficiency and effectiveness of the business is the organisation processes. Clarity of purpose and guidance, ease of use, smooth flow and clearly defined roles are essential in building a productive process. Processes are very much a way of doing things in order to achieve a given agenda or set of objectives. Over time, many processes can become entrenched organisational routines and be performed in a perfunctory manner. When a way of doing things or a practice becomes deeply ingrained, it becomes inflexible and forms a barrier to improving capabilities. As long as the status quo is maintained, improvements in capabilities cannot be made. It is only through an impetus to change the status quo that there can be improvements. This does not suggest that doing things differently will invariably lead to improvements. As the saying goes, improvements must mean change but change may not bring about improvements. In the Chinese context, one will do well to bear in mind that 'it is critical for companies to appreciate and respect Chinese cultural norms and practices and to align certain characteristics with management practice and organisational behaviour. Foreign-owned and multinational companies will find that trying to impose Western business practices and management techniques in China, which are typically more decentralised, direct and consultative, could damage employee relations, and create stress and frustration'. Herein lies the complexity of the issue. How does one know which practices will impact cultural norms and create resistance to change, and which practices are more susceptible to acceptance? This is where relationship and constant communications can go a long way to contributing towards making change palatable to the Chinese partners and employees. Both the partner and the employees must be enlightened on the need to create an atmosphere where there prevails an innate desire to seek changes that can lead to betterment for the business initially and for the workforce subsequently. In other words, people must feel aligned to the desired changes that are being sought.

Employee retention

Of the HR issues that were reported in the Mercer survey on M&A in China, employee retention is a dominant factor. The focus here is on a select group of talented employees whose contributions have a direct impact on either the company's profitability or its future. The objective is to connect this group of talented employees by engaging them to the new environment. This implies that the larger part of the workforce may not receive the amount of attention that is being accorded to talented employees. According to Mercer, value from emerging and younger Chinese organisations resides within its people and their relationships with others. Therefore, retaining talented employees after the M&A transaction is absolutely necessary. Underlying this is the need to first identify these key talents as part of the HR due diligence, first and foremost. The process of identifying these talents will be predicated upon a given set of desired competencies for each key position, on which objective assessments are based. Desired competencies will encompass both the functional and technical competencies as well as the behavioural competencies. The major setback in relying on a competencies-based assessment model to determine the suitability of Chinese managers is a cultural misalignment of management style, especially in a state-owned environment. Empowerment and the state-owned sector are necessarily non-compatible. How then will one go about defining competencies such as Chinese leadership? Will competencies be evaluated from an MNC perspective?

Once this aspect is successfully completed, the integration phase proceeds to the formulation of appropriate strategies to create an harmonious environment for newly integrated employees to work so that interpersonal relationships can be cultivated or existing relationships can be realigned, new processes and systems can be learned and observed and new objectives can be pursued.

Conclusion

In the past thirty years, China has transformed itself from an agricultural society of farm workers into the world's largest factory and economic powerhouse. The transformation began with the pioneer economic reformist Deng Xiaoping who was never worried about the colour of the cat as long as it catches mice and was always prepared to cross the river by using its stepping stones. The economic reform and development have lifted more than 400 million Chinese people out of poverty. According to the National Bureau of Statistics, the index of annual per capita net income for rural China is 798 in 2008 and stands at 816 for the urbanised areas from a base index of 100 in 1978. Notwithstanding this, income disparity of rural residents relative to the people living in urban areas is significant, creating social problems in modern China. As China grapples with more than a billion consumers, wealth distribution continues to be a major challenge in President Hu Jintao's pursuit of an harmonious society.

By using the stepping stones to cross the river, China readjusted and readapted its economic policies aimed at reforming private and stated-owned enterprises continually to transform the centrally planned society into a socialist market economy. The alignments and adaptations of economic policies and reforms created uncertainties and ambiguities, especially for foreign invested enterprises operating in China. The lack of clarity or transparency in interpreting business rules, regulations, and the law, particularly for foreign direct investments in mergers and acquisitions, may have influenced behaviours and practices that are presumably 'hidden' or 'unseen'. This has been occurring in the transition period when old and out-dated rules and regulations are being removed and replaced by newer reform policies and business rules. During the transition, greedy and corrupt Chinese businessmen may have taken advantage of the lack of business rules, and/or afford respect for adhering to its regulations.

Businesses in Westernised economies are generally conducted within a rules-based system under laws that are widely known and justly enforced. In contrast, businesses conducted in the Chinese environment are anchored in personal contacts and relationships. The Chinese businessmen have an aversion to formal, written contracts and prefer to rely on personal relations and social contacts with those in power to get things done. Chinese businessmen typically start with minimum written agreements and rules, leaving the rest to negotiation and oral interpretation as the business relationship evolves. Cultivating affective relationships by building guānxi is the first step in managing the human resource due diligence process in mergers and acquisitions transactions. An affective relationship constructed in social settings (guānxi) is unpacked into interdependent notions comprising human-heartedness (*rénqíng*) and affection (*gǎnqíng*); appointed trust (*xìnrèn*) and use or usefulness of personal trust (*xìnyong*); personality (*liǎn*) and face in society (*miànzi*). The importance of social exchanges of favours, the dynamic positioning of social hierarchies, and the intricate balancing of power are emphasised in M&A discussions and effective negotiations. In addition, the concepts of *HeQíng* (合情), *He Li* (合理), and *HeFa* (合法) form an integral part of the human dimension of the Chinese people. For the Chinese people, the law is not beyond humaneness.

Merger and acquisition activities are becoming more sophisticated and commonplace in Asia. For China, the developments of capital and securities markets, banking reforms and the adaptation of international financial and accounting standards to the market economy system attract massive direct foreign investment into the inner cities and the special administrative regions. The purpose for conducting due diligence is to uncover potential issues and unseen business risks by taking into account the legal, financial and human resource challenges. Specifically, human resource due diligence seeks to establish employment-related costs in an organisation, especially its unseen costs. The HR Due Diligence process may be grouped into three main phases: upstream, midstream, and downstream. In each of the phases, activities are explored and examined to determine if an exhaustive HR due diligence process has been conducted. Amongst the key factors are the formulation of appropriate HR strategies that are aligned to the business; the identification and assessment of HR risks of the impending M&A transaction; and management integration upon the conclusion of the deal.

The differences between the Chinese ways of doing things as measured against Westernised best practices are identified in the context of a due diligence process. These differences in work practice may be leveraged and harmonised by applying a standardised framework whenever HR due diligence exercises are undertaken. Using a HR due diligence framework, every situation or critical factor is examined in sufficient detail to uncover HR risks that would otherwise be left unseen. In most instances, the critical factors revolve around people management issues and people-related costs issues. From an initial conceptualisation, the four-step approach is driven from the organisational, legal, internal controls, and costs perspectives.

The concept of 'hidden' or, in many instances, 'unseen' is usually construed with untruthful intentions and/or bad behaviour. Contrary to popular beliefs, the notion of 'unseen', as espoused by the Chinese people, normally signifies truthful behaviour or acts that are tacit, unobserved, or remain unnoticed until uncovered by experience and relevant expertise. The notion of 'unseen' through the lens of the Chinese people is important as it highlights the significance of extending beyond effective relationships to understand what is truthfully unseen in assessing risks. The stages of the risk assessment process are risk identification, description, assessment and the formulation of a mitigation plan. Two risk assessment matrices – impact versus likelihood and manageability versus timeliness – are constructed to enhance the risk assessment process. Based on differing business conditions and the related business agendas for undertaking mergers and acquisitions activities, the relevant human resource strategies are explored and deliberated.

As soon as an M&A deal is sealed, human resource interventions are necessary for the handling and the taking over of the business. Integrating individual businesses from distinct national and organisation cultures and diverse ethnicity poses many challenges. The issues confronting management integration depend on the strength of the affective relationships of the parties, the thoroughness and comprehensiveness in conducting HR due diligence; the assessments to uncover unseen risks and the resolution of disputes in negotiations. The handing and taking over processes focus on the HR infrastructure, organisational and cultural integration, and the retention of talented employees.

What happens after the M&A deal is signed has important consequences. Cultivating an affective relationship with employees to build mutual trust and respect is essential. This is especially pertinent as management interventions are necessary to align organisation behaviour and practice to meet the goals and objectives of the merged organisation. Priority areas in change management should be addressed almost immediately and implemented within the first six months after the taking over of the business, and with available resources to manage the transition.

As China is growing rather rapidly in its key industries with an inflow of foreign direct investors, its cultural norms are gravitating from a relationship-based approach towards a rule-based business environment. As we navigate the dynamic web of guānxi and complexity in affection, the subtlety in communication skills for managing changes and face saving needs to be fully understood and developed. Protocol is important in a collectivist culture where the loss of face does not affect an individual but the group, and the community where the group resides. Cultural competence, including the interpretation of body language and of indirect clues, is a basic building block in change management. Regardless of the influence of foreign multinational corporate values on mergers and acquisitions, the importance in cultivating an affective relationship with employees is paramount in navigating potential employee relations matters. Considering human resource management matters at the various stages of the M&A transaction greatly improves the chance of success. Companies may minimise their exposure to risks by conducting an extensive human resource management due diligence before the M&A deal is signed.

Appendix: checklist for conducting a HR due diligence

(1) The organisation

    a. Organisational and departmental structure

    b. Composition of management committee, heads of departments, their roles and responsibilities

    c. Communities of *guānxi*.

(2) Authorisation policy and procedure

    a. Formulation of policy, and source of authority

    b. Limits of authority

    c. Approval process for expenses, purchase and Capex

    d. Bank signatories.

(3) Human resource budget

    a. Responsibility for preparing the budget and how this is constructed

    b. Breakdown of budget allocation to human resource department, other functional departments and business units

    c. Breakdown of costs allocation captured in human resource department, other functional departments and business units

    d. Audit of budget and cost allocations, such as recruitment costs to ascertain how costs are captured and budgeted for.

(4) Human resource information

a. Number of regular full-time employees, part-time employees, employees on fixed-term contracts, and independent contractors
b. Budget versus actual expenditure by department
c. Budget versus actual expenditure by grades and positions
d. 'Phantom' employees such as employees on secondment to/from other organisations
e. Benchmark existing headcount against industry norms, such as ratio analysis to determine excess employees for redeployment
f. Number of hours worked with reference to statutory requirements
g. Optimal allocation of the number of work hours per shift
h. Determination and scheduling of the number of work shifts per week.

(5) Employment documentation

a. Review human resource policy and procedure, especially the various provisions
b. Determine provisions that are obligatory and those that are the prerogative of management
c. Review letter of employment to detect variations to individual employment contracts, especially after the person is hired, and in particular employment contracts of senior employees
d. Investigate non-standardised terms of employment contained in employment contracts
e. Review special conditions and/or legal obligations for targeted employees
f. Investigate termination terms – check for 'golden handcuff or parachute' clauses.

(6) Salary management

a. Job structure and grading system
b. Comprehensiveness of job and position descriptions and the authority level of senior positions
c. Salary and benefits planning
d. Salary review and approval
e. Salary structure and its components
f. Statutory contributions as a percentage of salary, including a breakdown on types of contributions
g. Types of allowances, eligibility criteria and purpose
h. Definition of overtime, eligibility and computation of overtime pay
i. Bonus and incentive pool determination and eligibility
j. Trending of annual payroll to identify salary items not processed and/or paid through the payroll system
k. Cost allocation for transport and where these costs are captured
l. Cost allocation for festive gifts and reimbursement practices
m. Cost allocation of company functions and where these costs are captured
n. Group insurance and premium payments
o. Company uniforms and outfits
p. Leave administration documentation and archival process and storage.

(7) Training and development

a. Training needs analysis
b. Review of training plan, if available, to determine how the plan was created
c. Review of training budget, if available
d. Training as a percentage of salary costs

e. Review of training documentation and a breakdown of items captured.

(8) Union relations

a. Composition of union committee and background of union leaders
b. Review of collective agreement
c. Length and validity of each agreement
d. Arbitration history of organisation for the past three years
e. Pending arbitration cases
f. Union's participation in management meetings
g. Impact of collective agreement on employment contract
h. Management representation and experience of representative in negotiating with union
i. Responsibility for contributing to subscriptions and union fund.

(9) Shared services

a. Are there any shared services enjoyed by the M&A target SBU? What are these?
b. Where are these costs captured and what are the bases of the costs sharing?
c. After M&A, how will these be dealt with?
d. Is a transition period necessary?

(10) Principles of negotiation

a. No adjustments to terms and conditions to be made from the time M&A is made known
b. Ratification of minutes of meeting.

References

Abrams, L.C., Cross, R., Lesser, E. and Levin, D.Z. (2003) 'Nurturing Interpersonal Trust in Knowledge-Sharing Networks', *Academy of Management Executive*, 17(4): 64–77.

Aguilera, R. and Dencker, J. (2004) 'The Role of Human Resource Management in Cross-Border Mergers and Acquisitions', *International Journal of Human Resource Management*, 15(8): 1355–70.

Bond, M. (ed.) (1986) *The Psychology of the Chinese People*. Hong Kong: Oxford University Press.

Bower, J. (2001) 'Not All M&As Are Alike – and That Matters', *Harvard Business Review*, March, pp. 92–101.

Carleton, J. (1997) 'Cultural Due Diligence', *Training*, November, pp. 67–75.

Chadwick, M. and Zhang, L. (2008) 'The Importance of Due Diligence', *Ferriers Focus*: China, February *http:// www.google.com.sg/search?sourceid=navclient&ie=UTF-8&rlz=1T4SKPB_enSG284SG285&q—ergers+and+acq uisitions+in+chinaferrier+hodgson*.

Chan, K.W. and Tong, C.K. (2000) 'Singaporean Chinese Doing Business in China', in Chan Kwok Bun (ed.), *Chinese Business Networks*. Singapore: Prentice Hall.

Chen Jianxun and Shih Hui-Tzu (2008) 'M&As in China: Impacts of WTO Accession' *http://books.google.com.sg/ books?id=gT09g4KlD2UC&printsec=frontcover&dq— ergers+and+acquisitions+in+china&source=bl&ots=pXpA*

AS28X1&sig=6lE6TVCylXySYtbsE_JGqmDrioc&hl=en &ei=BSEfTeCSL9DQrQf-1qmJDA&sa=X&oi=book_ result&ct=result&resnum=8&ved=0CEEQ6AEwBw#v= onepage&q&f=false.

Chen, W. (2006) 'View from China', *CFO*, August 2006, p. 27.

China Daily website *http://english.peopledaily.com .cn/90001/90776/index.html.*

Chovanec, P. (2009) 'The Nine Nations of China', 16 November, pp. 1–3 *http://chovanec.wordpress.com/2009/11/16/the-ninenations-of-china/.*

Clisold, T. (2004) *Mr China.* Constable & Robinson.

Corwin, S., Weinstein, H. and Sweeney, P. (1991) 'Facing the People Issues of M&As', *Management Review*, April, pp. 47–50.

Davies, E. (2003) 'A Roadmap for China's Mergers and Acquisitions', *China Business Review*, July–August, pp. 12–17.

Fernandez, J.A. and Underwood, L. (2006) *China CEO.* John Wiley & Sons.

Harding, D. and Rouse, T. (2007) 'Human Due Diligence', *Harvard Business Review*, April, pp. 124–31.

Ho, C.K. and Koh, C.S. (2007) *"HR Due Diligence in a Chinese State Owned Enterprise: Exploring the tacit risks and employment costs in M&A"*, presented at the inaugural conference on International Business in the Asia-Pacific Region: Challenges, Opportunities and Strategies for Research and Practice', Beijing, China co-hosted by the International Business Research Group (IBRG), Monash University and the University of International Business and Economics (UIBE), China, 22–24 September 2007.

Hu, H. (1994) 'The Chinese Concepts of Face', *American Anthropologist*, 46: 45–64.

Kay, I. and Shelton, M. (2000) 'The People Problem in Mergers', *McKinsey Quarterly*, 4: 27–37.

Ke Fan (May 2006) *How Can MNCs Retain Their Employees in China?*, Cornell University School of Industrial and Labour Relations Center for Advanced HR Studies Working Paper 06–08 *http://digitalcommons.ilr.cornell.edu/cgi/viewcontent.cgi?article=1406&context=cahrswp*.

Lewis, P. (June 2002) 'New China – Old Ways', *Emerald Research Journal*, p. 11.

Lin, B. and Hung, S. (2006) 'Mergers and Acquisitions as a Human Resource Strategy', *International Journal of Manpower*, 27(2): 126–42.

Lovallo, D., Viguerie P., Uhlaner, R. and Horn, J. (2007) 'Deals Without Delusions', *Harvard Business Review*, December.

Luo, Y. (1997) 'Guanxi: Principles, Philosophies, and Implications', *Human Systems Management*, 16(1): 43–51.

Manpower China White Paper, *The China Talent Paradox* *http://us.manpower.com/us/en/research/whitepapers/china-paradox.jsp*.

Martin, J. (2009) *When China Rules the World*. Penguin Books, pp. 201–6.

Mayer, R., Davis, J. and Schoorman, D. (1995) 'An Integrative Model of Organizational Trust', *Academy of Management Review*, 20: 709–34.

Naisbitt, J. and Naisbitt, D. (0000) *China's Megatrends – The Eight Pillars of a New Society*. HarperCollins, pp. 2–7.

National Statistics Bureau, China *http://www.stats.gov.cn/english/statisticaldata/yearlydata/*.

Norton, P. and Chao, H. (2001) 'Mergers and Acquisition in China', *Chinese Business Review*, September–October, pp. 46–53.

Peng, M. (2006) 'Making M&A Fly in China', *Harvard Business Review*, March, pp. 26–7.

Perry, J. and Herd, T. (2004) 'Mergers and Acquisitions: Reducing M&A Risk through Improved Due Diligence', *Strategy and Leadership*, 32(2): 12–19.

Pye, L. (1982) *Chinese Commercial Negotiating Style.* Cambridge, MA: Oelgeschlager, Gunn & Hain.

Redding, S.G. and Ng, M. (1982) 'The Role of "Face" in the Organizational Perceptions of Chinese Managers', *Organization Studies*, 3(3): 201–19.

Rothenbuecher, J. and von Hoyingen-Huene, J. (0000) 'The Rise of Emerging Markets in M&As' *http://www.atkearney.com/index.php/Publications/the-rise-of-emerging-markets-inmergers-and-acquisitions.html?q=rise+emerging+markets+mergers+acquisitions.*

Rousseau, D., Sitkin, S., Burt, R. and Camerer, C. (1998) 'Not So Different after All: A Cross-Discipline View of Trust', *Academy of Management Review*, 23(4): 339–404.

Rovit, S., Harding, D. and Lemire, C. (2004) 'A Simple M&A Model for all Seasons', *Strategy and Leadership*, 32(5): 18–24.

Shen J (2004) 'Compensation in Chinese Multinationals', *Compensation Benefits Review*, 36(15): 15–25.

Shenkar, O. (2005) *The Chinese Century.* Upper Saddle River, NJ: Pearson.

Solomon, R. and Flores, F. (2001) *Building Trust: In Business, Politics, Relationships, and Life.* New York: Oxford University Press.

Swanton, M. (2006) 'Mergers and Acquisitions: China Creates New Hurdles for Foreign Investment', *Inside Counsel*, November, pp. 64–6.

Taylor, R. (2002) 'Globalization Strategies of Chinese Companies: Current Developments and Future Prospects', *Asian Business and Management*, 1: 209–25.

Tong, C.K. and Yong, P.K. (1998) 'Guanxi Bases, Xinyong and Chinese Business Networks', *British Journal of Sociology*, 49(1): 75–96.

Tong, S. (2007) 'Reforming State-Owned Enterprises', in G. Wang and J. Wong (eds), *Interpreting China's Development*. Singapore: World Scientific, pp. 123–7.

Vanhonacker, W. (2004) 'When Good Guanxi Turns Bad', China Europe International Business School, 1 April. *Harvard Business Review*, 18.

Wang, G. and Shirley, P. (2009) 'M&A in China – A Focus on Value: The Human Capital Factor', Mercer paper *http://www.mercer.com/referencecontent.htm?idContent=1343005*.

Wei Yu (2009) 'Party Control in China's Listed Firms', *Social Science Research Network*, January, p. 8 *http://papers.ssrn.com/sol3/papers.cfm?abstract_id=1326205*.

Winchester, S. (2008) *The Man Who Loved China*. New York: HarperCollins, pp. 8–65.

Xiao, J. and Zhang, T. (2005) *Investment: Merger and Acquisition in China*. Beijing: Foreign Language Press.

Yeung, I.Y.M. and Tung, R.L. (1996) 'Achieving Business Success in Confucian Societies: The Importance of Guanxi', *Organizational Dynamics*, 25(2): 54–65.

Zhang, M. and Stening, B. (2010) *China 2.0*. Singapore: John Wiley & Sons.

Index

Printed in the United States
By Bookmasters